About the author

After taking a degree at Trinity College, Dublin, Brigid McConville spent a year doing postgraduate work at Berkeley, California, and worked on the *San Francisco Review of Books*. For two years she freelanced in Dublin, writing for the *Irish Times* and *Irish Press* before becoming feature writer for the *Business Traveller*, when she was runner up in the Catherine Pakenham Award for young women journalists. Since then she has been writing books and freelancing for *Woman* magazine and the *Guardian* Women's Page amongst others. She lives in Somerset with her partner John and their daughter, Maeve, now aged two.

GW00584877

MAD TO BE A MOTHER

Is there life after birth for women today?

Brigid McConville

CENTURY

LONDON   MELBOURNE   AUCKLAND   JOHANNESBURG

First published in 1987 by Century Hutchinson Ltd
62-65 Chandos Place
London WC2N 4NW

Century Hutchinson Australia Pty Ltd
PO Box 496 16-22 Church Street
Hawthorn Victoria 3122 Australia

Century Hutchinson New Zealand Limited
PO Box 40-086 Glenfield Auckland 10 New Zealand

Century Hutchinson South Africa (Pty) Ltd
PO Box 337 Bergvlei
2012 South Africa

Typeset by Inforum Ltd, Portsmouth
Printed and bound in Great Britain by
Richard Clay, Bungay, Suffolk

British Library Cataloguing in Publication Data

McConville, Brigid
    Mad to be a mother: is there life after
    birth for women today?
    1. Mothers – Attitudes
    I. Title
    306.8'743   HQ759

ISBN 0-7126-1697-7

For Maeve and John

Acknowledgments

My thanks to the unnameable number of women who contributed their ideas to this book. In particular, Jane, Nicole, Gilly and Fay generously offered their experiences of motherhood. Sarah Wallace and her friends gave views from 'the other side'. My friends Lou, Hilary, Liz, Barney, Rachel and Jane have helped to bring this book to birth together with various 'Lambeth women'.

Julia Ryde and Penny Hall with their art therapy group for mothers revealed much about mothering. Carol McKeever and my sister Lucy gave me news from the Antipodes.

Thanks are due to my editors Gail Rebuck and Victoria Huxley for their ideas and enthusiasm, and thanks also to my agent Mic Cheetham.

Lyn Durward and Chris Gowdridge of the Maternity Alliance gave their valuable time and information, as did Hannah Corbishley of the NCT and Harriet Harman MP. I am grateful to VOLCUF, the EOC, the Workplace Nurseries Campaign and the National Childcare Campaign for their considerable contributions.

Last but not least, without the care and support of my daughter's childminder Heather Whitehead, her husband David and children Darren, Nicola and Mark, this book would not have been written. And without Maeve and John it could not have been written.

Contents

Introduction

I was mad to be a mother. I still am.

Our lovely, much-wanted Maeve was born in May two years ago. It's not so much that life changed, but that I saw for the first time what life is like for most women who become mothers in Britain today. It was a shock.

Like a lot of childless, professional women, I had enjoyed a world of independence, achievement, friends and colleagues. Suddenly I had no place in that world, and no knowledge of the world of mothers which I have since learned to grow into.

I wrote an indignant article in the *Guardian* women's page:

As much as I love my new daughter, who is funny and fat and bursting with enthusiasm, motherhood sucks.

I said I was baffled by the yawning gap between the congratulations one gets for having 'achieved' motherhood, and the complete lack of support for being a mother. Friends had visited, drank, presented flowers, admired the sleeping bundle – and then departed back to 'normal life'. It seemed as if they were disappearing into the sunset, and forever.

Where, I wondered, was the sisterhood of mutual support between women which had been our code of conduct for so long? We had learned that men oppressed women, at home and at work. But when I found myself cut off from the world of work by lack of childcare facilities and burdened at home by a new load of domestic labour, it seemed that I was on my own.

When I asked women for help, they said my man should do more. They were right, but he didn't change into a helpful, supportive father overnight. Besides, this was more than just a personal problem. I was stuck between the rock of feminist rejection of the traditional 'caring' role, and the hard place of a society which doesn't care for mothers either. There was a storm of letters from *Guardian* readers. Reactions took three forms, very roughly:

1. Why doesn't this whingeing/self-pitying/selfish/depressing B. McConville just pull herself together and get on with it – like I did. I had six children in a shoebox etc. and we survived.

2. How dare this anti-feminist fraud blame other women for her feeblemindedness. If she was brainwashed into bearing babies for the Patriarchy, that's her own look out. If her man can't cook she should try cooking him.

3. I know just how you feel. When I became a mother I too was broke, weary and isolated. My old friends didn't know me; my old job wouldn't have me. But give it time – there is a world of supportive mothers out there and the children are always worth it.

A few people sent me literature on how to get help for post-natal depression. Others rang me up and told me in fascinating detail how they are deeply repelled by birth, babies and breastfeeding. My family was tactfully silent. My friends with children agreed with me. Many of my childless friends were furious.

Clearly I had opened a can of worms. The explosion of feeling proved that here was an extremely sensitive and pertinent issue for women today, whether they are mothers or not. And I was pretty shaken by that explosion.

I wanted to look more closely at the ideas I had only touched on in the *Guardian*, to resolve my own dilemmas as a mother and a feminist, to find out more about how women felt about motherhood. I wanted to express a more balanced truth and to come to a mutual understanding with my childless friends.

2

By chance my publisher Gail Rebuck had just given birth to her first baby, Georgia. With one foot in the professional world and the other newly into motherhood she was convinced that we should explore the divides and dilemmas which confront women after the birth of children.

Many women were keen to help. They talked, wrote, revealed their experiences and feelings with candour and courage. Mothers and non-mothers alike, they strode out across the minefield. They wanted to point out the danger areas, lay claim to the no-man's-land of motherhood.

Women without children told how they viewed the state of motherhood and how they felt about old friends who had become mothers. Women with children told what it was like to enter a new incarnation as a mother – and how difficult it became to communicate with the loved ones of their previous life.

Mothers described how having children divided them from their former selves – and how they continued to experience motherhood as a division of their loyalties and feelings. Yet most women had paradoxically felt motherhood to be a healing force too, an experience which liberated and gave birth to unexpressed parts of themselves and which connected them to other women across barriers of time, class, age and race.

These personal experiences of motherhood weren't formed in a vacuum. The 'problems' which motherhood throws at women have as much to do with the society we live in as they do with the psychology and makeup of individuals. We live in a society which doesn't properly value women, and the exploitation, lack of power and low status that all women face is magnified in motherhood.

Mothers, like other women in other spheres of life, are victims of a glaring double standard. We are living in a time of strong ideological shoring up of motherhood. But the man-made ideal mocks at women who are compelled by economic and political factors to struggle to bring up their children.

What hypocrisy of our politicians to shed crocodile tears over 'the family' while they are scrapping the already puny

3

maternity grant and plunging more and more families into poverty. Governments pay only lip service to equal opportunities while it costs the average woman up to half of her life times earnings to have a family.

Every parent who ventures into the outside world with children knows that we live in a society that doesn't like them. Just the everyday business of living – from the design of homes, transport, leisure facilities and the health services to the very structure of employment – proves to mothers that the world is not organized with their interests at heart.

The undervaluing of mothers is linked to the undervaluing and abuse of children in this country. It's also part of a world-wide system of priorities which won't spare pennies to save children from starvation, but spends its pounds on stockpiles for nuclear annihilation.

These are the real reasons why women feel angry about motherhood. These are the reasons why women feel divided between love for their children and resentment of the burden which society puts upon them as mothers. Inevitably, women absorb some of the values of the society which undervalues women and mothers. But we didn't construct those values. Which is why everywhere, in endless different ways, women are working to support each other and to mend the divides of man-made motherhood.

I hope this book will be a part of that mending.

PART ONE

OTHERS AND
MOTHERS

CHAPTER 1

Views from the child-free zone

Divide and conquer

Warning: this chapter is biased. It contains the views of women who don't have children about women who do, and about motherhood itself. Some of them are childless without choice; some never want to be mothers. Some long to be mothers; others are happy to be childless. For all of them, motherhood represents a divide, separating their experience from that of women with children.

But isn't it wiser to gloss over the divisions between women, which are so often constructed to suit the purposes of those with more power than ourselves?

The views in this chapter are intended to be taken in the context of a whole book which is examining the dilemmas of modern motherhood from a woman's point of view. Many of them are balanced by the views of the women in the next chapter: women who do have children and who have felt the impact of the views expressed here.

How are we to get any closer to mutual tolerance and understanding unless we face and explore some of the misunderstanding and intolerance between us? Shedding a little light on what divides us and why, will I hope, help to defuse some of the frustration that we all do sometimes feel about motherhood.

This chapter is the first step in an exercise in looking at each others' points of view. And the exercise starts with the point of view of women without children, for whereas most of us sooner or later become mothers, there has been or still is a time for all of us when we are not.

And mother makes three

As non-mothers, there can be few women who haven't known that sense of disappointment which can follow a much-looked-forward-to meeting with an old friend who has suddenly turned into a mother.

Instead of sitting down for a long, uninterrupted talk – as in the old days – the new mother's attention is painfully split between the conversation and the needs of her child. Just when you feel you are getting somewhere, the baby (if it ever slept) wakes up crying for food, or a cuddle, or a new nappy – or from some obscure, entirely selfish need which its distracted mother tries desperately to identify.

Never mind, the old friends agree, they will meet again. But where? And when? It is difficult for the new mother to go to the pub or wine bar. She's not available to see a film or go to the theatre because the baby breastfeeds on demand. The best place seems to be the mother's home, again. Which, for the non-mother, probably means calling in after work – but that's when the baby has her bath, or suffers from evening colic, or when the baby's father wants to be with his wife and child. Of course, its not impossible to meet, but it certainly isn't as easy and spontaneous as in the old days.

Eventually the old friends (both feeling they have made a big effort to do so) meet again. The non-mother may have travelled across town or country to see her friend while the baby's father babysits for a few hours. Or if a single parent, the new mum may have paid for a babysitter – with the consequence that she has a meter ticking away scarce resources in the back of her mind.

For both of them, their relationship – by virtue of all the organization which went into their meeting – is already under pressure. As in a long-distance telephone call from a loved one, there is so much to say and so little space in which to say it.

Yet this is their chance to talk and the non-mother has much she wants to discuss – her friends, her job, her newly-made or just broken relationship . . . The new mother can listen and respond as she always has, but what has she herself to offer? The timing of her feeds? The nitty-gritty of nappy changing? The minute developments in her baby's growth? The round of chores – washing, cooking, cleaning?

These are precisely the kinds of subjects which the friends have scorned in the past. The non-mother tries to listen and take an interest, but frankly, she is bored. Worse, she suspects her friend knows she is bored. The seeds of tension and mutual misunderstanding have been laid.

Outside the magic circle

From the point of view of women without children it can often seem that – despite their efforts to maintain contact – they are shut out from the lives of mothers:

There is an attitude amongst women with children that their friends without children are no longer sympathetic to them. But my experience as a non-mother is that the women who had children tended to exclude the women who didn't have them. Friendship has so much to do with the passage of time. For instance, I want to spend more time with a friend of mine but she has to take her child to the doctor and so on.

Yet she's not apologetic. She doesn't say, 'Oh, it must be so boring for you'. It's just her job, what she does in the daytime – and it bores her too. It's a chore and there is very little to share.

Does this mean that a chore is not something that a woman should ask a friend to share? Is boredom such an enemy to friendship? This seems to be a crucial issue between mothers and non-mothers.

It certainly doesn't seem to improve a friendship when

mothers ask their childless friends to share in their 'boring chores'. Some women have no children as a matter of positive, well-thought-out choice, precisely because they wish to avoid the domestic drudgery and time-consuming tasks of motherhood. Why then should they take on the burdens of hard labour for someone else's children?

What seems to cause non-mothers particular offence is the assumption that may lie behind a request for help – that because a woman doesn't have children she cannot be busy. The corollary to this is an implied criticism that if the non-mother says she can't or won't help, it is really because she is a 'selfish' person.

Yet many non-mothers protest that they are channelling their energies into other absorbing occupations and commitments. A friend once told me how she had received an urgent phone call from her sister whose toddler had gone down with a virus. It was an SOS: would the childless sister please come to her house to help with cleaning and cooking that weekend?

As a kind-hearted sibling, she did so. But it still rankles with her that the whole family thought that she had nothing more important to do. In fact, the childless sister had to cancel several meetings with friends and colleagues in order to help out, and that at the end of a long working week.

Worse still, say some childless women, they are expected to be grateful for being 'included'. Some have told me of visits to old friends who now have children. Instead of the long walks and talks they were looking forward to, the new mums seem to have behaved as if their friends would enjoy nothing more than to play mum too. As this childless, lesbian woman put it:

I felt really angry and used by the time I left. There is an assumption that single, childless and/or lesbian women should feel gratitude for being allowed by some mothers to bath, dress, nappy change, play with their offspring. Yet I feel sure that my friend felt I really enjoyed the weekend and the kiddie-type activities.

Indeed, one furious non-mother complains that not only do

mums behave like this at home, but that they export their domestic chaos into other people's houses without regard to their friends' chosen way of life. To this woman it seems as if mothers are a self-satisfied bunch, trading on a spurious moral superiority and habitually using the pretext of watching children at play as an excuse to get out of doing any real work:

It would not occur to me to ask a friend who has time to sit in the park with her children or to visit friends for coffee to do my housework. It is however accepted that when visiting friends or on their visits to us I will undertake the lion's share of the work. Their presence is always required as mothers when the boring necessary work has to be done – cooking, washing up, cleaning etc.

I would not be considered a supportive friend if I complained of tiredness after a busy week and asked them to pull their weight. Yet over the years, as a result of visiting children, I have had to clean vomit, urine, excrement and foodstuffs from all surfaces. Never has a mother (or father) offered to pay for breakages. Very few have even apologized for their child.

Yet when staying with friends I always kennel my two dogs. Recently a friend we were going to visit for the weekend telephoned to ask if I minded not bringing the dogs as they would be untidy, noisy and disruptive. It did not occur to her that her three small children may have been just that on weekend visits to my home.

Is she just letting off steam? Maybe so, but it's scalding stuff. And from what women privately admit to, such strong feelings are certainly not uncommon.

Paradise lost: When Milton means bleach

Perhaps mothers who carry with them the whole package of family life are simply trying to include their friends in their new life. Perhaps they haven't really got any other option.

But when the mother's new life is dominated by tasks which are judged to be boring and menial, this can seem as if the mother is merely 'dumping' part of her workload on the childless friend. Maybe the mother doesn't experience this workload as dull, but this has much to do with the fact that she loves the offspring who are its beneficiaries.

But we don't all love all babies even some of the time. To some women, babies seem to be more like little animals than like human beings that one can relate to and care for:

I have nieces and nephews whom I am very interested in. But my interest in other people's children is, I'm afraid, extraordinarily small. I feel a bit about children as I do about animals: if they're mine and I'm close to them I might love them. If they are someone else's, unless I have good reason to, I don't.

In the interests of friendship, the childless woman may try to hide the deep lack of interest she may feel for the new person who has suddenly become the centre of her old friend's life. These are the kind of views she may keep to herself or share with other childless women, knowing that it will only hurt her friend to hear them:

It's very difficult to be interested in a young baby – although it's different when they get a bit older – unless you're in constant contact with them. A baby is a baby is a baby . . . unless it's yours. Not being a mother, as far as I'm concerned, it's a question of putting food in one end and clearing up at the other.

Although it is difficult for me as a mother to get the truly frank views of women without children on this subject, it is striking how often the word 'boring' comes up when the subject is raised. The painful truth for women on both sides of parenthood's Great Divide is that, to those without children, motherhood can be as intensely dull as it can be absorbing to those who have children. To the comparatively free and single, the happily married woman with a child is a person of no news.

Apart from the endless round of chores, some mothers have only a child's conversation to engage with. This may be fascinating to those concerned with child development, but to other adult women it means no gossip, no new ideas, no jokes. Yet many new mothers do remember how they felt about babies before they had any of their own. They may even admit – as mothers – that babies are boring:

I felt exactly the same way before I had mine – I really couldn't have cared less about other people's children. In fact, I dropped so many friends when they had children, because suddenly they became all embroiled in nappies. But now my interest has gone up – I look into other people's prams and all that . . .

Non-mothers tend to be critical of the women who seem to have forgotten that life – even for them – did once centre around things other than children. The 'magic circle' of mothers can look very exclusive when suddenly it forms up on a social occasion. I will always remember a party that I went to, where about twenty people had been invited for food and drink. Everyone was mixing well and conversation flowed merrily for an hour or so – until a new mum arrived with her two-month-old.

She laid a sheepskin rug on the floor in the middle of the room, and put her baby down to kick and gurgle. Within minutes half-a-dozen women had gathered around the child to talk about motherhood, while all the men and non-mothers drifted uncomfortably into the kitchen where they stayed until it was time to go home.

No doubt the front room was the warmest, most convenient and most sensible place to put the baby, and if the mother hadn't brought him she would have been stuck at home. But the fact remains that the child acted as the proverbial atmosphere Hoover, and our glum hosts could only watch helplessly as their party disintegrated.

Some women feel strongly that mothers should be more considerate about where and when they obtrude their preoccupation with children:

Mothers should have some discipline. They ought to accept that it is

13

a recently acquired interest for them, and not an interest at all to non-mothers. Yet if you go to a social gathering, often you find that the mothers have gathered together in a corner to talk amongst themselves.

Another non-mother, who says she chose not to have children because she was unwilling to accept the restrictions of motherhood, has reacted very strongly against mothers from her observations of their way of life. She can think of no single example of any friend's experience of motherhood which would make her wish for first-hand experience of it.

At the same time, she declares herself bored to distraction by the assumptions of certain mothers that everyone is fascinated by their experience and wants to hear every 'lurid detail' of their pregnancies, labour and subsequent lives with children:

It is mothers who self-restrict their conversation and who forget that it is only those who have experienced such aspects of life who want to hear about them. It's the difference between thinking of Milton as a poet and as a sterilizing fluid that separates the mothers from the rest.

Motherhood as a cop out?

To be or not to be a mother is a question that reaches beyond the social levels of friendship to strike right at the heart of a woman's sense of values. Its answer – wherever women have the choice – is one that reflects how women see the world and how they see their place in it.

When a woman chooses to become a mother, she is declaring her colours. The decision to have a child reveals in a very public way some very private priorities, emotions and values. Her choice can deeply affect her childless friends, forcing them to consider their own position, to reassess their own priorities, achievements and emotions. This can be a painful business. Sometimes the process can initiate a drifting apart of friends, and sometimes the parting is appropriate. The arrival of

14

children can crystalize differences between women that may otherwise have long remained dormant.

Does a woman see herself chiefly as a childbearer – or does she believe her most important role is in the outside world? Because of the way that home and 'work' are divided in our society, women face this artificial 'either/or' when they make their choices about motherhood. And when women give up their jobs to have babies – as many are obliged to do – are they saying to their women colleagues, 'the job is not the most important thing in the world' . . .?

For women whose energies are devoted to carving out a career, that's not a message they want to hear. For the woman who has spent a decade or more fighting tooth and nail to get where she is at work, opting for motherhood can look like a cop-out.

What is the point of proving that women can make it if women colleagues then opt out of their jobs to have children? From this point of view motherhood looks like a retreat into the home, and worse, into a life of servitude.

Professional women in particular are pulled in different directions over this issue. On the one hand, they are conscious that they may stand accused of collusion: are they buying into the values of competition and conventional 'success', values which many see as intrinsically damaging to women? On the other hand, it takes courage and determination to succeed in that world, and arguably women will never change that world until they carve their own place within it. Hence the guilty but honest ambivalence of this career woman who admits her old friend and colleague has, as a result of becoming a mother, ceased to have importance in the world:

I've got a friend with a child, and it's a terrible thing to say, but I don't rate her. Because she's given up, she's not competing. For me, at the age of thirty, competition is an important value. In terms of motherhood I know she is doing a great job: I can say that, but I don't feel it.

Ironically, this same emphasis on the importance of women

15

achieving equality in the world of work was a part of the reaction against traditional motherhood in the women's movement. In recent decades women have campaigned for equal pay and opportunities. The workplace became an important battleground for women. Sexual politics and the sexual division of labour were important too, but there was no heroism to be had as a housewife.

Yet because the male-dominated world of work was so effectively separated from the world of home, women were identified with one camp or the other. Only recently has the debate broadened, bringing new sympathy for the dilemmas of women who don't want to have to sacrifice either children or their work. The feminist magazine *Spare Rib* (January 1987) reflects this concern by looking back on feminist attitudes to motherhood during the '60s and '70s.

The issue became one of choosing, of what or who should be put first (job or home). By deciding, as women, to put ourselves and our liberation first there was a feminist backlash against motherhood. The 'wife and mother' stereotype was forcefully rejected and child-bearing and rearing became 'unfashionable' in many feminist circles.

In some ways this separated women from each other even further as those women who already had children or who wanted them felt that the women's movement 'disapproved'.

Opting for motherhood appeared to some as a retreat into the traditional women's role. And why choose such a role when women had at last won some rights to reject it?

For generations, feminists had been fighting for women's rights to control their own fertility. The rights to abortion and contraception have long been and still are fundamental in freeing women from domestic drudgery. For too long we had been 'lashed to our bodies' – in the words of the American poet and feminist, Adrienne Rich – and at last many Western women could enjoy the confidence of freedom from unwanted pregnancy.

Another fundamental tenet of the modern women's movement has been that we should exercise autonomy – not only over our bodies, but over all other aspects of our lives. It is a difficult ideal to attain, but many women have stood up for their right to determine their own sexuality, their relationships (or not) with men, for control over their own destinies, financial independence and so on.

Yet in the most obvious, but also the most profound ways, becoming a mother seems to be negation of autonomy. Suddenly the woman who swore she would never cook and clean up for a husband is servant hand and foot, twenty-four hours a day, enslaved to an infant in a way that not even the grossest male chauvinist pig would expect.

Not only has she abnegated her hard-won option to remain child-free, but she has probably lost her financial, social and domestic independence too. She can no longer go where she pleases, when she pleases, with whom she pleases. She is shackled to her pram, her nappy bag and milky breasts as surely as any wife of old was shackled to her oppressed role.

More important still, the mother seems to have lost her spiritual independence. A woman who would never have allowed herself to feel so dependent upon a man that she could not function away from his presence may – when she becomes a mother – admit to profound distress and desolation at being separated from her infant, even for a short time. Worse than the worst attack of being in love, she is obsessed by this new being; she can't think about, talk about, dream about or really care about anything else.

What happens to the idealism of some women when they become mothers? What happens to their liberal attitudes, their radical instincts? Suddenly the woman who was passionately opposed to private education and exploitation is employing a young nanny for low wages and sending the kids to boarding school, because it's 'best for the children'. It seems that motherhood divorces some women from their former ideals and weds them to the advantage of their individual offspring.

How do these aspects of motherhood appear to the women who have fought a hard struggle and made many sacrifices to win a new view of the world, to wean themselves from dependence, to defend the high ground of personal autonomy? Is it surprising if such women feel that surrendering to motherhood, especially full-time motherhood, is letting the side down?

Dupes of patriarchy?

There is suspicion too about why women want to be mothers. Since contraception has extended a woman's choice to be or not to be a mother, there has been some very rigorous examination into women's motives for having children. A whole book, 'Why Children?', has recently been dedicated to this question. It's a very modern question, and women are very sensitive about how it is answered.

I once wrote in a newspaper that I had become a mother for reasons that I don't fully understand, under the influence of forces that are beyond the range of consciousness, raised or otherwise. I was trying to convey what is really a very profound and complex reality for many women – the subtle mesh of influences that lead them into childbearing.

But some women thought they heard an echo of the patriarchal notion that we are frail vessels impelled by irrational and biological forces. As this non-mother wrote in reply:

In our vastly overcrowded world, in a society highly aware of the quality of life, 'wanting a baby' should be merely a starting point. Such desires are still heavily promoted as inescapable, when in fact our culture teems with other creative outlets that many women find more satisfying. Recognizing pro-motherhood propaganda is the beginning of coming to terms with our biological double bind: motherhood as our greatest glory versus motherhood as slavery.

Choices about childbearing must rest on understanding. Perhaps if mothers understand their choice a little better, it would be more difficult for the rest of us to dismiss them as dupes of patriarchal structures.

Some women who have chosen to be childless feel they have taken a stand against the traditional notion that it's 'natural'

18

for all women to want to be mothers. They are claiming a value for women which is wider than the old 'wife and mother' stereotype allows.

Fair enough. But this doesn't mean that any woman who wants to be a wife and mother is a brainwashed dupe. Ironically, it is a particular group of non-mothers who say they do feel an overpoweringly deep desire for children. That is, those women who desperately want to, but so far cannot, become mothers.

Childless without choice

Apart from women who have chosen not to have children, there are those women who have no choice in the matter. Current estimates put the proportion of infertile couples at up to one in seven. Many other women are without a male partner and don't wish to or cannot afford to bring up a child alone.

Some lesbian women take the option of artificial insemination, but they are the exception rather than the rule. Lesbian mothers also face a daunting barrage of social prejudice. Our legal system tends to assume that lesbians are unfit to look after children, and many have been deprived of their children.

Miscarriage too is a very common experience for women. According to some estimates, it is as common as childbirth itself. Yet it is not an experience that we – with our high expectations of good health and huge faith in modern medicine – are psychologically prepared to accept.

While it is considered 'natural' and 'normal' for women to give birth, a veil of stigma and taboo is drawn over those who 'fail' to do so. Just as we avoid the realities of death in our society, so we avoid the truth that not all pregnancies end in 'normal birth' of healthy children. In fact, one in a hundred women leaves the maternity ward either without a healthy baby or without a baby at all.

Because we don't expect to be infertile or to miscarry, because we aren't prepared for the early death or stillbirth of

19

children, or for the birth of handicapped offspring, such tragedies come with an added degree of shock. Women may feel like failures or deviants for producing a less than 'perfect' child.

It is an experience that can drive would-be-mothers into isolation and depression. The reserve of British people tends to put a stop on the expression of sympathy, and 'over-emotional' women are avoided with embarassment. As if she had committed some ghastly offence, a woman who is grieving the loss of her child may find that her former friends and acquaintances are avoiding both the subject and her.

A mother of a stillborn child told me how she felt like a pariah after she came home from hospital: she saw old friends crossing the street to get out of her path. She felt blamed for her own 'failure'.

Such attitudes can seriously widen the divides between women without and women with children. There can be few people who don't know someone for whom the whole issue of motherhood is considered a 'touchy subject'. And there is no doubt that for some women who are childless without choice, the presence of women with children, or news of someone else's pregnancy can be almost unbearable.

Even women who already have children can be devastated when a pregnancy is cut short:

Before my miscarriage I used to delight in other people's pregnancies – I thought, how wonderful, terrific. But afterwards, I couldn't bear to be told that other people were pregnant. I just felt an uncontroll-able, irrational and overwhelming longing for my own. I was amazed by the strength of it. I already had one beautiful child, yet I was experiencing this incredible desire for another. It just ruined every-thing. I was desperate.

Alone in a world of mothers

Many women who have had miscarriages describe the experi-ence as one of 'losing part of themselves'. Apart from the literal

20

truth in this, say Ann Oakley and her co-authors in their book *Miscarriage*, there is also the sense in which the lost foetus represents the fantasy of her future self:

[The foetus] is what could have transformed the woman into a mother, and the miscarriage has thus removed (albeit perhaps only temporarily) the woman's identification with the mother role.

It is typical, say the authors, to feel after a miscarriage as if one is alone in a world of mothers.

This sense of loss can last a lifetime. One woman told how she went through a depression at the end of the summer. It was eleven years after her child would have been due, and in her imagination the would-be mother saw her child starting secondary school.

For others, family occasions such as Christmas are permanently shadowed by sadness at what might have been. One friend, now a mother of two, has told me how even the mention of pregnancy would send her into floods of tears after she miscarried, and how she feared for a while that she might snatch a baby from another woman's pram.

In our society, such loss is not accorded any real weight. It is not dignified by any recognized ritual, as death is by the funeral ceremony. Women are expected to grieve in isolation, to 'get over it' quickly. They may be told by well-meaning people and medical staff that they can 'have another one', as if this will eradicate the whole tragic experience.

An insidious notion further aggravates the suffering of women who have lost their children. It is that they are not 'real' women until they are mothers. Our society expects women to become mothers: this is the 'natural' thing to do, and a woman is not fully mature until she has 'achieved' motherhood.

Not only is this terribly damaging to a woman's sense of self, it may open painful divides between their childless state and the lives of her friends who are mothers. This is how a member of the National Housewives' Register, writing in the organization's magazine, reflects on her own experience of infertility:

It is possible to survive, but never to recover from, the knowledge that one has failed to fulfil the basic requirement of all living creatures – to reproduce . . . The reality of the problem only hit me when I discovered a newly pregnant friend was unable to tell me her news because she did not want to upset me. The failure one feels is grinding.

My parents have no grandchildren, my dear husband has no baby of his own to love. I have this love in store to give to my child – love that cannot be used in any other way. I need to be loved and needed by my child, and I shall never be 'grown-up' as I shall never make the transition from being someone's child to being someone's parent.

Yet we lack nothing, and one day when I tell my nappy-burdened friends of some treat we are going to have or expensive purchase, I shall not have to qualify my news with those pathetically apologetic words '. . . of course, we can only manage to have it because we don't have children.' (*NHR Newsletter*, no. 38)

It may not occur to a mother that a childless friend may secretly think of herself as pathetic, unnatural or not fully adult. Nor that she feels the need to apologize for her existence. It may not occur to a woman who doesn't want children either.

Women without men

In no less insidious ways, women who are keeping their options open about children and who are living without men may suffer from the same assumptions about what is normal for women. For them the social penalties of childlessness are linked to the stigma of being 'on the shelf'.

There is a die-hard, male chauvinist notion that all a woman needs to keep her satisfied is 'a good man' (usually put more crudely). Bed-fellow to this, is the idea that a childless woman who works hard at a career – or anything else for that matter – is merely sublimating her deep-seated desire to have children.

Perhaps such a woman does have a deep-seated desire to have children. Perhaps not. Either way, her childless state should not be used as a way of denigrating the positive and creative ways that she does use her energy. Nobody asks if the workaholic man is sublimating his deep desire to be a father, even though many men do long for children and may be starved of emotional warmth and closeness.

Lurking behind such judgements against childless women is the old attitude of 'a woman's place is in the home' – the right place for her to express her inborn 'maternal instinct'. She can't really be happy in her job (the thinking goes): that's just a temporary way of keeping her busy and earning pin money until she meets her man and starts her family. Besides, ambition is not a trait which is considered becoming to women. Indeed, it is often seen as a warped expression of the unfulfilled desire to have children.

In her book *Femininity*, the American writer, Susan Brownmiller describes how ambitious women are widely regarded with dread. From the 'ballbreaking' career woman of American mythology to the 'pushy mothers' of Hollywood starlets, ambition is a characteristic which – in women – is seen as threatening, embarassing, inappropriate and damaging.

Brownmiller points to how ambitious women have been depicted in literature: significantly, many of them are childless. Furthermore their ambitions are dangerous, even perverted, and this is linked to their childless state as if they have been driven to desperate extremes by their 'barrenness'. There is Lady Macbeth, a driving force behind her husband's murderous ambition. She not only has no children, but she also curses mother's milk and maternal tenderness. There is the destructive Hedda Gabler, and the legendary Madame Defarge who sits knitting beneath the guillotine, perverting that feminine symbol of creativity just as a witch perverts the function of the housewife's broomstick.

If there is a conventional 'right' way for women to direct their ambitions, it is not into politics or worldly power (even Mrs Thatcher has no other women in her cabinet), but into forming relationships, finding a man, building a family. It's a way of thinking that's unlikely to change until women's position in society is radically altered.

23

Men do still hold the reins to money and power, and until that changes there is of course going to be intense pressure on women to find Mr Right and bear his children. For many women, happiness, security and status as they are publicly perceived still depend upon getting married and having children.

Perhaps it is less true for young women today than for their mother's generation, but women are still made to feel failures if they don't get their man. It is a message we are bombarded with daily through the media and through advertising; from buying booze to choosing toothpaste it's finding a mate that matters. Having a child is evidence of having 'succeeded' in that competition.

Consider the word spinster, in all its connotations of being dried up, unwanted and unattractive. There is no equivalent word that puts men down for being single. Bachelor, by contrast, suggests a rich and rakish existence, free from the clutches of a wife. Feminists have tried to 'reclaim' the word spinster and give it back its positive sense (it originally meant an independent woman who earned her living by spinning thread), but it is still widely used as a derogatory term for single women.

For the state of living without men and without children is 'different'. It is even a threat to the established social order. To go manless and childless, and still to survive and be happy: this implies that men aren't necessary, that women need not be independent upon them, that motherhood is not the only source of fulfillment! Revolutionary notions indeed . . .

Jumping on the bandwagon

Yet some childless women would like to live with a man and to have children, but don't because they have never met a man with whom they could have a close and committed relationship. Women's expectations of relationships have gone up with their financial independence, and while they may feel justly proud of maintaining high standards, the burgeonings of other people's children may nonetheless be a galling reminder of their unwanted single status.

Of course, some mothers can come across as a real pain in the neck, parading their babies in full regalia as if no one else ever had one. No doubt they are expressing their pride and delight in their children, but to women who are hurting from the lack of a child, this may seem like smugness and self-satisfaction.

How irritating for a woman who doesn't have the opportunity to 'take a few years off' for her young family, to be faced with a new mother who is free from the necessity to compete in the big bad world.

For a while is seems as if mothers may have opted out of competition, they have also – in another respect – won THE competition, the official, male-sanctioned Women's Event. It's as if we all start off at the beginning of the race together. Some women strive (manfully?) to keep to the fore, only to find that the mothers have left the race – but are being applauded and flattered for having done so.

A friend once told me that while she was glad for my sake when I became pregnant, she also felt somehow abandoned and rejected by me. As a single, childless woman in a heterosexist society which is geared to the lives of couples, she felt that I had 'jumped on the bandwagon', leaving her to struggle on alone. This is despite the fact that she has a career, income, home and circle of friends that anyone would envy.

Another friend, with an enviable record of achievement under her belt, told me that she still felt she hadn't done anything lasting. If she could have a child she thought she would feel fully 'capable', that she had created a life for posterity. At the back of many women's minds too, is the prospect of their old age, which they fear may be lonely in the absence of children and grandchildren.

The wider family network, based as it is on the regeneration of the generations, is a particularly difficult context for a woman who is unhappy about being manless and childless.

Within this circle women feel they are being compared with their other female relatives, and when sisters (especially younger sisters) and cousins are having babies, the pressure and criticism can be painfully intense.

It's not just that 'success' in the world is not always entirely rewarding, but that friends and relatives may not really rate it as important in a woman's life – at least not as important as getting married and having a baby. Just how happy and satisfied the women with men and babies are is beside the point: it is the expectation of what the role may bring, coupled with social pressure to be a wife and mother that can grieve the childless woman and divide her experiences from those of a mother.

Taking out shares in motherhood

But why should it be only those women who give birth who have the right to the mother role? Don't we all, including men, have the capacity to love and nurture children, irrespective of our biological relationship to them?

There are plenty of societies in which children are cared for not primarily by their biological mothers, but by their grandparents, their aunts and uncles, even by their brothers and sisters. It has been quite common for West Indian parents to leave their children with grandparents while they went to find work abroad to earn enough money to send for their children. In African societies too, children are commonly 'fostered' by relatives.

Yet in Britain the demarcation between mother and non-mother remains strict. Just because a woman isn't a mother doesn't mean she's not fond of children, or that she has no talent for getting on with them. Sadly, she may not get much opportunity.

As Naomi Pfeffer and Anne Woolett write in their book *The Experience of Infertility*:

Mothers and non-mothers often seem to inhabit different worlds. Infertile women often long to join the world of mothers but feel that because they lack the credentials of having a child they would be viewed with suspicion. Mothers may envy the childless woman her freedom and perhaps her relative affluence.

Women without children often fear that they do not know what to do, that children will not like them, or that they will over-compensate and look foolish. And mothers may find it difficult to understand that another woman wants to look after her children, or she may feel threatened that another woman might be more skilful in looking after her children.

The other side of this coin is the thrusting of babies upon childless women, as if to say: 'Here, it's good for you to find out what its all about.' Childless women friends have told me how they dread that visit to the maternity ward to see the new baby of a friend or relative. Invariably the child is handed over, while a silent question reverberates amongst the onlookers – 'When are YOU going to get on with it?'

This is not only embarassing but unfair, as women without children are rarely given the opportunity to spend time and learn confidence with children. The idea that a child will be damaged if it is parted – even for a short time – from the woman who gave birth to her, is very strong at most levels of British society. (The upper classes have always exempted themselves from this rule with the system of nannies and boarding schools.)

It was after the war that the writings of the influential psychologist John Bowlby were used to put the fear of 'maternal deprivation' into mothers. Mothers were expected to be the one and only true love of their infant's life – with some exceptions made for fathers.

This idea, however, as Anne Dally points out in her fascinating book *Inventing Motherhood,* is a modern, Western one which – far from being divinely ordained – is a by-product of the way our social institutions operate. In her researches she has found no other culture which assumes as we do that the biological mother has exclusive care and responsibility for her babies.

It is history and economics which have separated the world of work and power from that of the home and delivered it into the hands of men, leaving women at home as the isolated caretakers of children.

As recently as the last world war, economic necessity led to a huge workforce of women emerging from the home to work on the land and in the factories while their children were cared for by the state in nurseries. But as soon as the war was over and the men wanted their jobs back, the nurseries were closed and women went home to care for the children – and to be consumers of the new household products which flooded the market.

Today's mothers, despite the fact that many are also working in the outside world, are still seen as prime carers in the home. This system saddles mothers with a double shift, while cutting non-mothers off from contact with children, and because there is such pressure upon mothers, they tend to claim exclusive rights to the loyalties and affections of their children in return.

But biological reproduction is not the only route to the mother role, even in this country. With divorce breaking up a third of UK couples, many women and men are finding themselves in the position of step-parent in a newly formed 'hybrid family'. Many women who have never given birth thus find they are nevertheless someone's 'mum'.

In feminist circles there is discussion about whether non-biological 'mothers' can share in the mothering role. Ideally, there seems no reason why they shouldn't. But will today's mothers, who have to make such sacrifices to have children, relinquish power and control? In the real world we have a long way to go before childless women can feel secure in the knowledge that the love and care they may extend to someone else's child may not be suddenly rejected and the child arbitrarily withdrawn from them.

This is the view of a childless, lesbian woman who does not want to be cut off from relationships with children, but who has cause to be concerned about her own vulnerability in relation to mothers:

Very early on I made the decision not to become involved with any women who had children, because of the power of mothers. Yet when my sister became pregnant and decided on single parenting I realized that here was a situation in which it was possible for me to become deeply involved with a child, without the risk of arbitrary withdrawal of access, simply because of the blood ties between my sister and myself.

For this woman, the fact that society recognized her relationship with the child as that of aunt gave her an additional sense of security. This is important both for the aunt, and for the child, who has an established way of naming her and of understanding the relationship to her.

Other childless women whose close friends become mothers say they are tremendously pleased and proud when they have been asked to be godmothers. Here is a formal, established way of sharing the mother role, in some of its aspects at least. Of course neither godmothers nor aunts have the right of access to a child, but at least they have a socially recognized status as women with a special and caring relationship with a child.

The Great Divide between mothers and non-mothers is by no means uncrossable. Many women are very happy to remain without children, finding their fulfilment in other forms of creativity, making relationships with other people's children. Others become mothers themselves in time, rejoining old friends in a new way of life.

CHAPTER 2

Views from the 'other side'

The great sea change

Becoming a mother heralds for many women profound changes in themselves and their way of life. Indeed the changes are so unexpectedly deep that mothers often talk in terms of 'being in a fog' or 'feeling submerged' for months after the birth – feelings that are only partly to do with the physical changes and tiredness of life with the newborn.

On almost any occasion of profound change women talk to each other about what is going on, putting difficult feelings into words, bringing complicated events into focus. Sickness and health, falling in and out of love, the dramas and desperation of divorce, death, work and family life – most women know that somewhere they have a loyal female friend who will sit and listen and respond to how they feel about the basic patterns of existence.

Yet there is one such basic pattern – the business of becoming a mother – which is almost impossible to communicate to women who haven't been through it themselves. The new mother with her small bundle is herself a soul beginning a new incarnation. Like her own newborn, she is in a strange world, learning a new identity, struggling to locate herself, testing faculties and senses for the first time.

Many a new mother would love to be able to tell her friends of what has happened to her. She needs and wants to discuss it, to help sort it out in her own mind as well as to include other women. But just as manifest as the physical presence of her baby is the divide that has suddenly opened between the mother and the non-mothers. Having crossed to the 'other side', she finds it a source of mystification and grief that she can't communicate with those she loved in her previous life.

Now perhaps for the first time, the new mother becomes aware of just how segregated our society is, and of how isolated mothers can be. If she lives in a city and had a job before her child was born she probably mixed with other contemporary, probably childless people. Her world was the world of paid work, colleagues and peers. Apart from her immediate family, she may have never mixed with anyone much older or much younger. Perhaps she has friends who had children before she did, but the chances are they drifted apart, and she may never even have held a baby until her own was born.

Suddenly the new mother finds that she no longer belongs in the world of the non-parent. She is cut off from her colleagues in the office. She can't go out to meet her friends unless the expedition is well planned and coordinated with babysitters. But more troubling than the practical difficulties are the emotional gaps that have opened between herself and her old friends.

The secret love affair

The feelings that mothers have for their newborns are nothing if not complex and contradictory. But at the positive end of the spectrum many women say they experience a kind of emotion – some compare it to an intense and passionate love affair – that they have never known before. They are totally, painfully, vulnerably, ecstatically infatuated with their new baby.

Yet there is a taboo about talking about this aspect of motherhood. Sally Emerson, in her book *A Celebration of Babies*, suggests that this is partly because women don't want their husbands to guess their devotion to the new loved one in case they become unbearably jealous:

So the kisses and hugs are kept private and only the complaints made public. Women know they are being unfaithful to their husbands as they lie with their babies kissing and cuddling and singing words of love. The men have little idea that these tempestuous affairs are going on in millions of houses.

Sally Emerson is indignant that she had only been told about the negative side of motherhood, of the broken nights, endless nappies and screaming children. With such a grim view of the whole business she might very well have missed the whole experience and with it the unprecedented depth of love, sense of wonder and renewed faith in humanity that her child has brought her.

Nobody told me that babies were wonderful, challenging and in a day supply more information about the ways of mankind than could be discovered in a year of study. Only one person told me about the passionate love affair between mother and child, but then I didn't believe her . . . Why did nobody admit that babies were such extraordinary pleasure machines, that the losing of self in love for a baby was as exquisite as the losing of self in love for a man?

Who else would a woman lose so much sleep for but for a lover – or a newborn? Who else could invade her every waking moment and (in her limited sleeping ones) her dreams? To what other voice but that of her lover – or her baby – would a woman's body respond so rapidly, so automatically?

As a society we have become so obsessed by genital sexuality that it's difficult for us to feel relaxed about the range of sensual delights which children can bring. When women's breasts are Page Three material, on daily display for the sexual delectation of men, it can be hard even for a woman to remember that breasts are also for feeding babies.

So when a woman discovers that breastfeeding her child can be a pleasure, how does she mentally disentangle the 'sensual' (permitted) from the 'sexual' (taboo) and talk about what she feels without fear that she is confessing to a strange perversion?

Babies are delectable creatures, with warm, tender caressable bodies. They invite kissing and cuddling, for after all they are totally vulnerable and dependent on making us love them. There can't be many mothers who haven't wanted playfully to 'bite' the little round arms and legs of their babies. One friend told me how she wrestles with her urge to 'bite' her little boy's bottom every night when she takes him out of the bath.

Yet all too often we project our adult notions of sexual desire and behaviour on to our attraction to children, and worse, on to children's innocent explorations and touchings of us. One day our sixteen-month old daughter toddled up to another mother, put out her hand and touched her on the knee. 'If she's a girl,' this woman said, in all seriousness, 'she shouldn't be doing that.'

Such British hang-ups about physical contact, together with our limited vocabulary of love, stunt communication between mothers and the rest of the world. It's alright for a modern woman to describe how she fell in love at first sight with a man. Such tales are the stock in trade of the vast industry of television, film and printed fiction. But to tell of falling in love at first sight with a baby? Such experiences may be talked about in some circles, especially with the post-Kitzinger emphasis on maternal emotion, but they are hardly the common currency of our culture.

Perhaps in this hard age of individual achievement mothers sense that it is considered soft and unliberated to 'lose oneself' in love for a child. Not only is this a sin against the 'Me generation', but it sits uncomfortably with the thinking of the women's movement, which has long encouraged us to value personal autonomy and independence.

It also somehow seems tactless, if not meaningless, to try to communicate such an experience of love to a person who has not herself known it. Just as we are more reserved about discussing love affairs with people who are reluctantly celibate, so mothers sometimes feel they should hold back what they feel from women without children. For who can tell whether another childless woman is not yearning for a child of her own?

Such a gap in experience can open divides between even the oldest of friends, as happened with one new mother after fifteen years of closest friendship:

The friend I do feel separated from is the one who I know longs for children. I do still see her and there is still a great bond between us, but I cannot begin to share with her the great joy I feel in my children because I know it would just carve her up. For me motherhood has been such an overpowering experience that I am very sad not to be able to share that with a friend with whom, up until now, I've shared virtually everything.

Moaning about motherhood

Far simpler than singing the praises of your own newborn is to complain about the burdens of motherhood. It will be true – at least some of the time – that the new mother is exhausted, fed up with nappies, bored with feeding and wiping, irked by the treadmill of shopping and cleaning. She may feel that – in terms of the values of her previous life in the 'real' world – she is turning into a mindless drudge: when did she last read a paper, express an informed opinion, share an uninterrupted evening of adult company?

This is something that a new mother can talk to an old friend about, because the conversation refers to the values of the world which the friend still inhabits. The account of her sufferings will give the friend an opportunity to respond with sympathy. After all, domestic drudgery is something that most women know something about, whether they are mothers or not.

However, ultimately, moaning about motherhood is a self-defeating form of communication, and not an entirely honest one either. Who wants to be this stereotype of a miserable mum, the bearer of bad tidings, and 'horror stories' to put the wind up other mothers-to-be? It's also pretty boring for a friend to hear too much about a mother's trials and tribulations. Besides, she's probably heard it all before – and not wanted to hear it – from her own mother.

Isn't this kind of one-track whinge also a betrayal of the mother's true, complex feelings about the whole rich, rewarding and frustrating state of motherhood? Isn't she in a way offering the old friend an olive branch, saying, 'You're not missing out on as much as you might think . . .', although really she feels that her friend may be missing out on a great deal?

There's also a penalty to pay for giving oneself such a bad press. All mothers are caught between the idealized image of glowing Motherhood and the Valium-blanketed stereotype of the harassed, if not hysterical, mum. By self-confessedly not living up to the impossible ideal, women may be labelling themselves as failures as mothers.

A mother who dwells too much on the negative aspects of her experience risks being talked about as 'neurotic', unable to cope, lacking in 'natural' maternal instincts. That's bad enough in itself, but it has further perilous possibilities in this time of rising public awareness of child neglect and abuse.

And what do *you* do?

Paradoxically, at the same time as privately knowing they have a most fascinating new role, mothers also get the message loud and clear that our society simply doesn't rate motherhood. Moreover – despite a lot of hypocritical cant – it doesn't like children. As non-mothers we have all heard – may even have joined in – the chorus of groans when babies came up in conversation. We know from the past that for anyone who isn't a mother, motherhood is widely considered a very 'boring' subject.

Many mothers say they have been dropped by childless

friends as soon as they gave birth, sometimes even while pregnant. The recent mother suspects, with reason, that her old friends are finding her new life baffling if not downright dull. When they call her up for a chat, how can she explain that after repetitive tasks of childcare there isn't even enough room in her life for sleep, let alone stimulating new events and ideas? Their enquiries force her to ask herself if she really is becoming a bore, and also to admit to herself that elements of motherhood are intensely boring:

My friends who don't have children are doing things in the world every night – going to films, to the theatre, to dinner – all the sorts of things I used to do before I had a child. They ring me up and talk to me for ten minutes about what they've been doing, and then they ask – what's been happening to you? I say, well, I went to work, and I've been looking after the baby. What more can I tell them about? Not work – they'd be bored. The baby? I could say 'she pushes herself up more than she could yesterday', or 'now she holds an object for two minutes as opposed to one.'
But I just don't think they'd be interested. I personally would not have been interested in what I had to say before my own baby was born. So I feel an insecurity – that I have in fact got nothing to say to them. I'm sorry but I haven't done anything in the world. I haven't been to a film, or the theatre . . . or had an emotional upset, or broken up with a bloke. I have told them the baby did this or that, and I get this silence, followed by . . . 'oh, how nice . . .'.

Motherhood is so seriously and systematically undervalued in our society that mothers do often feel themselves and their role to be insignificant and mundane. Even as children we learn – from observing our own parents – how motherhood just doesn't figure in the workings of the outside world, the 'real' world as it is commonly called – with quite insulting connotations for home life.

A GP who is also a mother, was hoping – but not optimistic – for the position of partner in a medical practice. Her family commitments had meant that she had passed the age of forty without yet being able to take on such a job. In the course of discussing her hopes around the kitchen table her teenage daughter suggested she should introduce herself to a plastic surgeon.

'What for', asked the mother? 'To have a face lift, iron out a few wrinkles, lie about my age?' 'No, no', said the daughter, 'you could get him [sic] to put a large scar down the side of your face. Then when you went for your interview the panel would think – "Well, she must have done something interesting in all those years while she hasn't been a partner!" '

Not only did this girl assume that her mother's colleagues would not rate motherhood as valuable, but she did not perceive the bringing up of herself as an interesting achievement. So even as children we absorb the knowledge that mothers aren't valued, and we perpetuate the process by undervaluing ourselves and each other. It's a vicious circle from which it is not easy to escape when it is daily and regularly being reinforced in none too subtle ways.

Even after decades of modern feminism, when some people assume that women have already 'got equality', it's quite commonplace for men to put women down for being mothers. Despite having been employed as a social worker for years before she had children, this mother initially found it hard to defend herself against male disdain for her role:

I went to a dinner party and was seated next to a man who would be considered a success in the world. Once he found out that I wasn't working [sic], that was it. He didn't talk to me, he had already pigeonholed me. I made a few unsuccessful attempts and just had to sit there boiling up, unable at the time to say anything about it.

But since then – when were out for the evening as a couple – we were introduced to a man who immediately turned to my husband and asked him 'What do you do?' I challenged him and asked him why hadn't he asked me that. We managed to treat it in an amusing way, but I could see that it had made him think and I was pleased about that.

Of course the undervaluing of motherhood is part and parcel of the general undervaluing of women in our society, and Australian writer, Dale Spender has shown how in mixed company women are expected to listen and respond to male conversation, despite being labelled as the ones who 'rabbit', 'gossip' and 'natter'. But mothers have to bear the double put-down of knowing that – as well earning minus points for being female – no one really wants to know about their low status, unpaid, 'boring' and menial work.

Talking shop

Those who don't want to hear about motherhood and children tend to argue that it's talking shop, and talking shop is boring. There is some truth in that, and no doubt there are individual mothers who could bore anyone to death with details of their infant prodigy – but they would probably bore people on any other subject too.

Many mothers would say this is a thin excuse for avoiding the painful truth – that as a society we don't treat motherhood as a respectable activity. Compare a gathering of any other breed of professionals: a group of doctors at a party will talk medicine, lawyers will talk law, journalists will talk news and gossip. That's also talking shop, but (as long as the individuals aren't bores themselves) no one will complain about it.

In contrast, mothers know that in mixed social company it is frowned upon to discuss their 'jobs'. As a result they have to resort to statements like this, in order to keep their end up:

I've often said 'I'm a housewife and a mother, but I'm still a very interesting person'.

Imagine a professional man having to plead for regard in this way:

I'm an architect and a father, but I'm still a very interesting person.

The view of motherhood as unskilled and uninteresting is also enshrined in the thinking of employers and officialdom. After a year of receiving unemployment benefit following the birth of her child, a Somerset woman was asked to fill in a form so that her benefit could be reviewed. One question on the form asked, 'Have you learned any new skills since you were last employed?' She wrote 'Motherhood' in the appropriate space. Having sent the form back to the DHSS she received a telephone call asking her to delete the word 'motherhood' from this section as it couldn't be considered a skill.

Even in the context of other women's activities which are widely regarded as unimportant or frivolous, motherhood has a low status. In recent years feminists have won regard (amongst women at least) for the practise of meeting in women-only groups. From the women-only policy of the Greenham Common peace camps to women-only publishers, consciousness-raising groups, bookshops, restaurants and parties, the exclusion of men signifies that women together have something special and valuable to share.

In contrast, there is no 'right on' status for women at their mums' and toddlers' groups, mothers' coffee mornings or playgroups. The exclusion of men from these gatherings is not seen as an assertion of strength, but as the natural consequence of women being expected to mind the children while their fathers are out at work, 'real work' that is. What these women are up to is no more than – pernicious term – a 'mothers' meeting'.

Sisterhood after motherhood?

No woman who becomes a mother in the 1980s is unaffected by the women's movement, whether she calls herself a feminist or not. Yet there is a tension between feminism and motherhood today – and the relationship has never been a simple one.

Ideas about motherhood in the Western world have varied as much as the issues of feminism over the past few hundred years. Different times and circumstances have elicited different views and responses from women, and as Ann Dally points out in *Inventing Motherhood*, it is only comparatively recently that women have thought there may be a 'problem' in motherhood and childcare:

What the early feminists wanted was legal rights, opportunities for education and self-fulfilment, and acceptance by society as people in their own right . . . It did not occur to the early feminists that the raising of children would create problems. Childbirth itself might be a problem because it was so frequent and hazardous, but there was no problem about the care of the children once they were born. There were plenty of people willing to look after them and able to do so by the standards of the time. It would not have occurred to people that children needed special provision for play or stimulation, or that they needed the constant presence of their own mothers for several years from birth onwards . . . It is doubtful whether many children were ever looked after exclusively by their mothers until the present century.

Many of the feminists of the last century were married women with children who saw motherhood as a vital and fulfilling task. Early American feminist, Elizabeth Cady Stanton, had seven children. For her, as for most middle-class women up until the present, the solution to domestic ties was to employ a trusted housekeeper who cared for the home and children while their mother was busy elsewhere. Women like these hardly realized that motherhood meant loss of freedom for their less fortunate sisters, because they could afford servants to preserve their own liberty and leisure time.

Yet their privileged position did not stop such women from pointing to the isolation of mothers in the home as the source of their ignorance and lowly status. Stanton and her colleague Susan B. Anthony wrote in 1881 in *The History of Women's Suffrage* that 'a mind always in contact with children is necessarily dwarfed in its proportions.' To escape their stunted and stultified state, they believed, women must be identified first and foremost as women, not as wives and mothers.

It's a sentiment that is not at all out of place in today's feminist thinking. Of course, women wish to be perceived as the individuals they are, rather than as a man's wife, or a child's mother, significant only in their supporting role to other people.

Unfortunately, that argument, while based on a belief in women's equality, comes confusingly close to the patriarchal view of mothers as third-class citizens, which is based on a belief in women's inferiority. It is not feminism which undervalues motherhood – but it is feminism which points out that undervaluing. Mothers don't want to be ignorant or of lowly status, but they don't enjoy being called ignorant or lowly either. It's a situation which calls for skill and tact, for no one likes the bringer of bad news.

Motherhood on the margins?

The women's movement is not a single, uniform entity. Women have myriad concerns which they express in many different ways, and which change with time and events. However, the divides between mothers and non-mothers crop up in the various groupings of the women's movement, just as they do in the rest of women's lives.

New mothers who have been involved in the women's movement before their babies were born may find – just at the time when they are likely to feel most vulnerable most isolated, most cut off from the world of work and friends – that the groups they once felt at home in have little to offer them in their new role.

A glance at the listings in feminist magazines or at the billboards of a women's centre reveals a common set of themes. Such issues as contraception and abortion, peace, racism, rights for disabled women, the oppression of lesbians, together with campaigns to win equality for women in the world of work have been to the forefront in the 1980s. The difficulties faced by single parents and by lesbian mothers have also been on the agenda, but given the fact that some eight out of ten women are mothers, motherhood has had a surprisingly low profile in the more visible and vocal areas of feminist concern.

41

Rather than seeking to emphasize the true value of mother-hood it seems that many women have been voting with their bodies. Much of our generation has reacted to the low status of motherhood by choosing to have few children or none at all. Indeed, so unattractive has motherhood become to women today that the demographic experts are worrying about our population dwindling away, and Germaine Greer has written at length about our 'anti-child Western lifestyle'.

Consistent with this generally gloomy outlook, some mothers have complained that they feel alienated by a passive hostility which radiates from women who otherwise see them-selves as allies and supporters of womankind. One such mother who took her baby, plus a helper, to an Open Universi-ty women's studies' course went home disillusioned:

I could not cope with the conflicting demands on me as a mother and as a student. My fellow students offerred me no support, neither moral nor practical. At the time I imagined I was paranoid in believing I was on the receiving end of some passive hostility. Now I am not so sure. I know that I went home feeling I would have experienced more sisterhood amongst women in a terraced back-to-back at the turn of the century.

To its credit, the feminist magazine *Spare Rib* has taken up the issue by giving mothers space to air their grievances. One mother wrote to say that she had found:

most feminists quite unconcerned with the work of mothering . . . [Others] who did not strongly disapprove ranged in their reactions from sympathy, through questioning my sanity, to changing the subject.

In the past feminism has come to the defence of women who have had no choice but to reproduce, and has criticized the media for propagating society's assumption that all women want to have children, but as this mother puts it, there is no point in throwing out the baby with the patriarchal bathwater:

There is a massive gap in the women's movement where the politics of mothering should be . . . It's not enough to campaign for reproductive rights. We must consider what we do with the end products of reproduction – babies, children and young people of both genders . . . We need to be considered when you plan conferences and bops . . . Some of us need breastfeeding space where we can be comfortable and relaxed with our sometimes vocal babies. Some of us want our children with us at meetings, readings and discos. Space must be made for us.

I want to know why women with ten-year-old sons cannot take them to Horton [peace camp], and don't expect me to accept the same crap I get from the landlord of the local pub when he asked me and my child to leave. I need support to challenge attitudes like that.

Mothers united

Happily for mothers, the tide seems to be turning. As the women who discovered feminism in the early '70s are reaching their late thirties and having children, motherhood is becoming an important issue for many a vocal old activist. Through the women's committee of the late lamented GLC came strong and committed support for childcare projects throughout London.

In public life, women like Harriet Harman, the Labour MP for Peckham and mother of three small children, have been drawing attention to the lack of childcare facilities not only at Westminster but nationwide. In formerly radical communities in the USA too, like Berkeley in California, motherhood is definitely in the ascendancy. *Spare Rib* has begun to publish a page on 'Parenting', and *Everywoman* regularly carries features about parenthood.

Certain feminist writers (who are also mothers) like Adrienne Rich, Ann Oakley and Betty Friedan have become well known over many years for their contributions to this debate, analysing the institution of motherhood and how it oppresses women. In the arena of health, too, feminist thinking has been

43

influential as women have fought for greater say and control in how and where they give birth.

Meanwhile, mothers as a group – feminist and not – have long been organizing for their mutual benefit. From large national organizations with a relatively conservative profile – like the Women's Institutes and the National Housewives' Register – to more radical pressure groups like the Maternity Alliance, the concerns of mothers have been the concern of other mothers.

In the long tradition of mutual support between women, the National Childbirth Trust (NCT) organizes groups for women before and after they give birth; and all over the country mothers club together to run mums and toddlers groups, playgroups, toy libraries and community nurseries. For the many mothers in paid work, a good childminder is their invaluable support and ally.

Yet feminist though this broad spectrum of women may be in its achievements, it's doubtful that many would identify themselves with this label. Much blame can be laid at the feet of a male-dominated and hostile media coverage of feminism for giving the label a bad name, but this is not the only reason why a large proportion of women in this country, many of them mothers, don't feel comfortable with contemporary feminism.

Of course, the vanguard of any movement is at some remove from those it claims to speak for. Until motherhood and childcare become issues which are more widely regarded as important in the women's movement, it seems likely that mothers will continue to feel that 'feminism' isn't addressing their needs. Yet it's quite possible to narrow this gap too.

Recently, Black and ethnic minority women have asserted themselves and pointed out the racism amongst white feminists. Older women and lesbians have made their voices heard and pointed out ageism and heterosexism where they have cropped up in the women's movement. Disabled women have established that they too must be included or the women's movement would be mirroring the oppression they claimed to oppose. The women's movement has listened to and accommodated these women's voices.

Woe betide the women's event these days that doesn't advertise its accessibility or not to disabled people. Sisters Against Disablement (SAD) protested outside the Feminist Bookfair in Covent Garden when they found their way blocked by flights of stairs. But how many women's events advertise access for prams and buggies, facilities for feeding and changing? Increasingly there seems to be an awareness of the need for crèches, but we still need to raise our awareness of mother's other requirements.

Mothers have not yet had their full say. Is there a language to express the conditions of motherhood? Housewife is even a dirty word amongst the women of the National Housewives' Register who are changing their title as a result: and we have no such terms as 'motherism' to dignify our condition. Yet the kind of prejudices mothers face are not very different in kind from those faced by older women, Black women, disabled women, lesbian women: mothers too find themselves to be powerless, invisible, and exploited.

Arguably, women don't experience the full oppressive extent of patriarchy until they take on that most common of women's roles in motherhood. It is in this role that we feel at first hand just how much we have been living in a world created by men for men, how much our freedoms and independence can be curtailed, and how our society is structured to keep us in a position of isolation and dependency. It's a role which, perhaps more than any other, needs a feminist analysis and needs the understanding and support of other women.

Why mothers are muted

So why aren't the mothers shouting louder, demanding more, making the headlines? The women's movement has taught us that one of the most insidious aspects of oppression is that the oppressed absorb the values of their oppressors and don't see themselves as oppressed.

All we have to do is to accept the common assumptions of the day and we are undervaluing ourselves as mothers. This is the view of a mother of four, who has found that many mothers – perhaps to ensure their own survival as wives – adopt the judgements of the people they are often dependent on, their husbands:

The lack of status in motherhood manifests itself in subtle ways and many women demean their jobs as mothers without even thinking about it. They run around catering for their husbands' needs because 'after all, he works hard at the office' (what about that blissful, totally uninterrupted sleep on the train, I say!)

It's also hard work to get women to bring their husbands along to an NCT social: 'Well, he thinks we're just a bunch of mothers discussing the latest nappies.' These are the same women who will quite happily find a babysitter, buy a frock, put on the lipstick and go to their husbands' firms' 'do' – and listen to the gossip there. His job matters – ours is dispensable. His job has economic value – the value of ours is not so easily assessed.

Mothers are also muted by their isolation in the separate units we call home. Unlike other workers who gather at their place of work, mothers have little opportunity to develop a collective consciousness or to take collective action – although this has not stopped them from trying. There are also the factors of sheer exhaustion and lack of time to organize anything but their families and households – often at the end of a day spent working for wages. As one disappointed mother wrote to me, at the cost of being late for her child's playgroup:

Many women have little voice in women's issues but yet greatly deserve to be heard. Unfortunately as the women's movement well knows, changes in attitudes require a great deal of time and effort by the pressure groups seeking them. These two items are fairly non-existent among mothers.

So what about the rest of the women who aren't mothers? Should childless women take up the cudgels for women with children? Is it realistic to expect women who have chosen not to have children in order to avoid the burdens of motherhood, or women who aren't heterosexual, to be advocates for women who choose to be mothers and to live with men?

Before my child was born it never occurred to me to examine the situation of women with children. Like women who got married, I somehow assumed that mothers had set themselves apart, that they had their own support within the family. Only mothers know, and therefore only mothers can say, how much they do need and want support. Let's hope the rest of the women's movement will keep its ears open to what mothers do have to say.

Who cares for the carers?

A particularly thorny issue for mothers is that of asking other childless women for practical support. In the post-natal period, a mother may feel overwhelmed by tiredness and the drastic changes in her life. On a practical level she desperately needs the help that in other times and other cultures was supplied by grandmothers, sisters, aunts and friends. But in the absence of this support network, can she turn to the network of her women friends?

This is very problematic when the help a mother needs is classified as housework or childcare. Feminists argue that women must beware of the attitudes which assume we are the 'natural', the only carers. Too often the notion that we are biologically better suited to taking care of others has allowed men to shirk their own responsibilities.

At home, men have expected women to cook and clean and take care of the family. At work, women are concentrated in the caring professions – like nursing – where they are expected to take on huge burdens for paltry salaries, because they are women. When the state fails to provide welfare and health services for the sick, the very old and the very young, it is women in their caring role, who are expected to stay at home to look after them.

Feminists have long been challenging this kind of thinking and insisting that it's time men did their fair share. Excellent in theory. But in practise – as most of us know from experience and as periodic women's magazine surveys have shown – men don't do anything like half the housework or childcare. Of course they should, but to date, they don't. There are some glowing exceptions, but their women can count themselves amongst the fortunate minority. And as well as the many women who live with a man who doesn't pull his weight, there are many single mothers living without men.

So who can a new mum turn to, in the confidence that her request for help won't be resented? Perhaps her own mother, if she is around. But is it fair to ask women who were obliged to give up their own working lives in bringing up this generation to take care of our children so that we can go out to work? What about her women friends? Isn't that also a case of asking other women to take on the caring role, a role that feminists have been working to reject?

Unless the new mother is asking for help from another mother whom she knows will reciprocate in kind, the ideals of sisterhood can find themselves in headlong collision with the needs of motherhood. Between the man who should support her and doesn't, and the woman who says 'ask him, not other women', today's mother all too often has the choice of the rock or of the hard place.

A male conspiracy?

The fact that most mothers are, or have been, involved with men as the fathers of their children, as the sharers of their homes and sometimes as their closest companions, tends to set them further apart from the more radical strands of the women's movement. At one pole of feminism are the separatists who see any involvement with men as undesirable. It's not a widely held view, but women are still on the defensive in fighting for their rights and some don't like or trust men whom they see as responsible for their oppression.

48

There is no doubt that the majority of men don't do nearly enough to share the domestic burdens of their women. Many men don't even think of motherhood as work; work is what *they* do, an important function which earns money. Perhaps women ought to leave such men. Perhaps many women already have: it is women today who are seeking the majority of divorces.

But there are millions more who can't or don't want to leave their men – for reasons of 'love', money and the ties of children. What these women perceive as anti-male pressure often aggravates the conflict they already feel, and fails to endear them to the anti-male lobby. You don't have to believe in any conspiracy theory to see that such divides and misunderstandings between women operate in the interests of men.

When a woman has a baby she places herself in an extremely vulnerable position. More than ever before in her life she is likely to be financially dependent upon the support of her man – as well as being emotionally and often physically vulnerable too. She needs his help, support, commitment and understanding. Not only her women friends but common kindness dictate that he should share her burdens.

If he won't help her what can she do? She may refuse to accept his behaviour, confront him with her demands. But as one mother who survived much isolation, abandonment and general indifference writes, her bargaining position is not good:

Men don't help because at present they can get away with it. When a woman loses power by becoming a mother she is badly placed to push her man too hard. If she does he will either seek a more accommodating mate or spend his time in the less demanding company of his male peers and 'unchilded' women.

She may decide to take the initiative by leaving him – but while such a move may salvage her self-esteem, in practical terms it often means jumping from the frying pan into the fire. Life for the single mother is rarely a bed of roses. Instead of not

49

enough help, she often has no help. She is also joining the ranks of the most poverty-stricken group in our society.

Men's economic power enables them to escape from women who expect them to share in parenthood – and to attract new women with that same economic power. Motherhood for many women becomes a trap, in which they serve not only their children, but their man. Non-mothers can only find out about this situation by listening to mothers. For women not to know about some of the harsher realities of motherhood plays very well into the hands of men who exploit women, as this mother believes:

It is supremely in the interests of any patriarchal system that young childless women should not 'know'. We as mothers must establish a continuing dialogue with single women. The next time any single woman fleetingly resents the demands made on her by any mother she should ask herself – in whose interest is this division? Where should my resentment properly be channelled?

Surely it must be channelled into changing the institutions which maintain power in the hands of men at the expense of women.

There are individual men who want to be part of this process of change. Ironically, it is when a mother is living with a man who shapes up pretty well to feminist standards of behaviour, a man with whom she has a close and mutually supportive relationship, that generalized anti-male feeling is particularly alienating.

One mother, whose husband stays at home much of the time with the baby, says that she is turned off by the 'scathing contempt' which some feminists seem to have for all men. She feels he can't win. Either he is treated as a macho pig, or as a wimp:

Few if any women that we meet in the course of our work believe that he does his fair share of looking after house and baby. If he dares to turn up minus child he is interrogated about whether I've been literally left, chained firmly to the sink, with the baby on my hip. On

50

the other hand, the reaction to my working is one of congratulation – well done, you've conned him again! I'm sure many people who don't know my husband see him as a cartoon character: four foot tall, thinning hair and a perpetually eager-to-please expression on his face. They tend to treat him as if his presence is an intrusion, his conversation an irrelevance.

New beginnings

Airing the differences in our perceptions, looking critically at the issues that come between us – these are things we have to do to understand our dilemmas as friends and as women, as mothers and non-mothers. But what next? What can we do about them?

Most women do adjust to the enormous changes that children bring. The younger the child, the more intense the sense of dislocation seems to be, but time softens, ameliorates, compensates for that sense. The feelings of mutual loss between friends are most severe when a tiny, speechless – but amazingly noisy – baby is devouring its mother's energy and attention.

In time this baby turns into a small person who can communicate and make friends with the mother's old companions. The small child may still be demanding, but she is also likely to be affectionate, funny and delightful. Meanwhile, the friend without children may come to be especially valued precisely because she is a source of information about the world of work and provides the opportunity for much-craved conversations about anything *other* than kids.

There are also compensations in the realm of new relationships. In her former life the mother may never have known her near neighbours, but only a small and like-minded group with similar interests and background. Now, however, she is in regular contact with a much wider cross-section of women who just happen to be mothers too.

From the time of her first ante-natal class, through post-natal groups, mums and toddlers groups, playgroups and into the school years, she has the opportunity to meet women whom she may never otherwise have encountered. The occasions that bring mothers together cross barriers of class, age, race and temperament. Motherhood has a universal quality which links women to a great range of contemporaries, and which – as this mother points out – brings out the finest kinds of empathy in women:

My seven years of motherhood which included twice moving to a new area, have been made bearable and enriched by the ready support, help and friendship of other women at home. For a new mother of a young baby there is no one like a person in the same situation to understand and share the burden of childcare, particularly if relatives live a long way away. Of all people in society, a young mother is admirably placed to make contact with a wide cross-section of women able to provide staunch and loyal friendship and support.

Paradoxically, there also is a positive spin-off from the awfulness of not being able to communicate about one's life to non-mothers: it is that other mothers know just how isolated you are likely to feel:

I don't regret the years that I have given to my kids, even though there were times of great frustration, anxiety and boredom. I enjoyed the commitment – it's the biggest one I'll ever make. Like many other new mums, I got through those first few years with an informal network of friends all in the same boat – you share a very special intimacy with your female friends at this time.

The new links of motherhood spread from women in the local community to total strangers stopping on the street to admire the baby. In spite of a strong anti-child element in British society, there are also thousands of individuals who smile when they see a child and go out of their way to help a struggling mother.

The presence of a baby also gives men an opportunity to express publicly the gentler side of their natures. The fact that many men are tender-hearted fathers allows them to show goodwill and attention towards women with children – without the niggling sexual overtones which so often bother women in another context.

What woman wouldn't be cautious about being invited out of a train corridor to sit alone with the male steward in the first-class restaurant? Yet when his motive was to spare me the indignity of changing my baby on the corridor floor, this man gave me cause to reconsider my curses upon British Rail.

Explanations are tiring

Above all, as many mothers discover with experience, it is mothers who are best equipped to help each other. Not only do they know what it's all about, but mothers can offer each other the kind of reciprocal help that women can't when only one is a parent. One mother can go shopping while another takes care of the children, and then vice versa. Not only are they doing each other good turns without need for guilt, resentment or embarassment – they are also providing playmates for their children.

There's much to be said for the cheery attitude of the mothers who think it's a waste of time to mourn the pleasures, friends and freedoms of a past life. Far better to look forward with good humour and make the most of a period which – arduous though it may be – doesn't last long. This is the advice of one seasoned mother who freely admits she found young motherhood difficult at the time:

We are singularly ill-prepared for this supremely important role, and we only get one crack at it. So forget about going out to the pub, unless you can get a babysitter. In a few years you will appreciate its baby-free state. Instead, take the carrycot and bottle of vino along to the home of other young parents. Shift the toys and crumbs off their arm chairs and share your frustrations with them. Admire the cobwebs on their ceilings and consider how little they matter. Even if you have no more than the childrearing state in common with other parents, they will afford more comfort than friends without children, because they will know how you feel. Explanations are tiring.

Much of this shared experience and mutual support brings mothers full circle into a renewed recognition of feminist values:

I am proud to describe myself as a feminist. The experience of motherhood has made me love and admire women even more than I did before. Women, I believe, endure. First we endure childbirth – most of us deserve medals for coming through such agony! Second, we endure the burden of motherhood which is the result of lack of adequate provision for mothers with babies and children in society.

Motherhood also links women with other women across time: remembering our own mothers, reliving our own childhood, going through what women have always gone through. In quite a profound way, the experience of providing love and care for a baby can stir our own childhood memories. After the span of post-adolescent years in which young women often pull away from their own mothers, it's a humbling experience to be plunged into the total commitment of motherhood and to realize with a jolt – 'this is what my mother did for me'.

In her novel *The Good Mother*, Sue Miller writes about a mother watching her three-year-old daughter being enfolded by the love of her own grandmother:

As a family I think we must all have been marked by the diminishment of love with time and age because of that pure lost bond we had all shared with Gram. And I felt now . . . the sense we sometimes have as adults of living things again through our children, of restoring to ourselves those things we've lost, of giving ourselves those things we've never had.

On a deep level, motherhood spans the divides of time to connect us back to earlier generations of mothers, and links us also to the mothers of the future.

CHAPTER 3

Divided from yourself

Babyshock

To many women in our society, the reality of motherhood comes as a shock. For months, even years, most women await the 'happy event', wrapped in pleasurable fantasies of the love, warmth and tenderness that they will soon share with their newborns.

Once the child is born, the mother is initially buoyed up by attention to the baby and visits from friends and family members. Surrounded by gifts and flowers she enjoys a rare sense of celebrity. The nurses and health professionals have probably been kind and helpful – for the first week, at least.

But after that week what happens? The well-wishers disappear back to 'normal' life – their jobs and unfettered friends – and she is left on her own, all day, every day, with the baby. With only her babycare books to turn to (unless she is lucky in her friends and family), she struggles around the clock to do her new job in which she has no experience and which she may never have seen anyone else perform.

In time, she may discover – or create – her own support system. But ask her how she feels a few weeks or months after the birth and she is likely to say, 'Nobody told me it was like this'. A sense of let-down, anti-climax and depression is so common in new mothers that it is treated as a 'natural' phenomenon to get the 'blues'. Of course, most new mothers feel exhausted and depleted by the demands of their twenty-four-hour-a-day dependent, but post-natal depression has more complex sources than hormonal imbalance.

For the new mother is not only having to come to terms with the divide between the person she once was and the one she is now, but with the divide between what she expected from motherhood and how she is discovering it to be. Within motherhood itself she is experiencing a whole series of conflicts – in the demands made upon her by her baby and her man, in her ambitions to be a good mother and also to remain a creative individual – and in her feelings for the new child itself.

Pregnancy is no preparation

The announcement of pregnancy is traditionally a time of celebration and congratulation – yet these days a lot of women dread becoming mothers. Hence that comical moment when you tell a friend you're pregnant without having told her if you want to be: her face freezes in uncertainty between the ritual expression of joy and a ready look of sympathy.

If you put her out of her misery and tell her you do want the baby, she might suggest breaking open a bottle of champagne . . . until she remembers that alcohol is not good for you in your condition, and becomes the first of the well-meaning throng of people who are going to advise and admonish you to take care of yourself – for the sake of the baby.

As soon as your pregnancy begins to show, perfect strangers will tick you off for lighting a cigarette, tut tut if you raise a wine glass to your lips, admonish you if you climb a step ladder or lift more than a shopping bag. Health workers and a deluge of literature will direct every aspect and advise on every limit to your lifestyle, from lovemaking to moving house. From months before you conceived you were supposed to have prepared your body, the breeding ground, with diligent 'pre-conceptual care' in order to provide the best environment for the good health and development of your baby.

Never did you experience so much solicitude until you became a childbearer. But now you have a clear, nine-month vocation: you must diligently attend classes, memorize breathing exercises, visit the ante-natal clinic, eat well, put your feet up, get plenty of rest, stay calm, keep yourself looking good – and of course, generally relax and enjoy being a mum-to-be.

All this will no doubt help you through the hour of birth – but it couldn't be in starker contrast to what happens from then on. For the *next* nine months you hardly go anywhere, are too tired to remember anything, only have time to pick at congealed baby food, never get a decent night's rest, feel like a zombie – and whatever you wear ends up a banana-smeared, milk-dribbled mess.

This mother of two looks back to that time with a mixture of anger and resignation – anger that no one had told her what the difficulties would be, yet accepting the near-impossibility of conveying those difficulties to a woman who hasn't yet experienced them:

There was a great build-up of 'How wonderful! You're going to have a family!' Then when the baby came, the attention was all for the baby. I was left in the background, feeling absolutely knocked sideways by the physical effects of motherhood. That was a shock. I was out of control. Looking back, I don't think you can spell that out to people. If you could, half of them wouldn't have children.

All in all, pregnancy is not just a lousy preparation for parenthood. It is, in total, an utterly misleading contrast to the reality of life after the baby. Indeed, as health visitors and husbands disappear off into the sunset leaving the new mum with her week-old stranger, perhaps an unworthy question drifts across her weary brain: what was all that fuss and care and attention really about . . .?

Sugar and spice, all things nice

In the small, often divided, families of modern Britain it's not at all unusual to meet new mothers who have never even held a baby before their own were born. With no younger siblings or cousins to practise motherhood on in the past, it may well be the case that a woman's sole experience of nurturing a small loved one came from playing with dolls when she was a child.

Playing with dolls is a way of teaching girls what mothers are supposed to do, while dividing them entirely from the realities of the job. As Ann Oakley points out in her book *Housewife*, doll play revolves almost entirely around servicing activities – washing, dressing, feeding, tidying the doll's house.

Yet a doll, however much she may live in the imagination of a child, is not a living, demanding creature. A doll can be dropped and forgotten about at any time. A doll will not howl for hours; a doll will not wake her child 'mother' night after night; a doll will not soil and wet and puke.

Nor does playing with dolls prepare a girl for the often overwhelming physical changes and demands of motherhood. As the new mother sits up painfully upon her stitches to breastfeed her baby in the post-natal ward, her nipples sting and her womb aches. This is a far cry from tending the plastic dollies of her past, and it is strangely incongruous with the romantic congratulation cards and flowers around her bed. Only now does she discover that physical discomfort and disruption to her body is an inevitable part of motherhood for a long time after the birth.

The shock of motherhood seems to be a peculiarly Western phenomenon. Just as we have lost contact with the realities of death in our society, so we have removed birth from the family home and neighbourhood midwife and made it into a hospital affair to be dealt with by distant professionals.

By contrast, many children of the developing world learn what it's all about as they mother their own living baby brothers and sisters and cousins. Today's women are perhaps as sheltered from the facts of motherhood as our grandmothers were from the 'facts of life'.

Nobody told me

So why don't women simply tell each other what it's going to be like? Some women think this is a conspiracy of silence. One grim mother snorted with disdain at the memory of her hospital ante-natal classes:

They never put first-time mums in with those who've already been through it in case it terrifies the beginners too much!

I didn't believe her and decided that she was probably a little depressed, if not paranoid. Within months I was asking other women with children – 'Why didn't you tell me?' Invariably, the answer was 'I did, but you didn't listen.'

One mother of four went through the same process and resolved to warn her own friends:

I've since taken two friends aside, before their first baby's birth and told them. Afterwards they said 'Why didn't you tell me it was like this?' My mother says that once you are pregnant it's too late to change your mind so why put a damper on it – the reality catches up soon enough!

There does seem to be a kind of selective deafness amongst pregnant women: just as we can't truly remember past experiences of pain, we can't envisage a future with the baby that is anything but rosy. According to Hannah Corbishley of the National Childbirth Trust, an 'appalling vacuum' develops in the lives of many mothers from the time they give birth until their baby reaches about eighteen months:

Before birth some very unrealistic, idealized views of motherhood are put across. Women imagine their new life with a gorgeous, pink bundle – and then mothers are left with a crying monster.

It is part of the task of the NCT's ante-natal teachers to bridge this gap, but, says Ms Corbishley, women won't listen:

However hard we try, our teachers tell us that women simply don't hear it. Maybe this is nature's way of protecting us: we can't take this information on, we have to get through the business of the birth first.

Nature certainly gives babies precedence over mothers in terms of their physical needs, depleting the mother's body of nutrients if necessary to feed the foetus, and it seems as if the same laws operate on the psychological level. Women's contentment during pregnancy is bought at the cost of much emotional depletion of the mother after the birth, as this mother of four discovered:

Having thought that the child would be my fulfilment I found the loneliness excruciating and simply didn't know how to go about overcoming it. It took me months to realize that my old friends really were only superficially interested in my new life and that I had to go out and find new friends – i.e. women with babies.

Fortunately I had a good Health Visitor who encouraged me to contact the NCT and I started going to coffee mornings and made friends. However, those few lonely months left quite a scar. The adjustment to this new role is, I'm sure, made much easier if there are women around with whom one can share the experience.

Too deep for words

Yet there is more to the silence around motherhood than selected truth and selective deafness. The same women who say they felt shocked and unprepared for the realities of motherhood suggest that the change is too profound to explain to people who haven't been through it, too deep to put into words:

The deep chasms that opened up, the deep questions, I just wasn't prepared for. I felt very conned into it – although my mother had been very helpful and said, 'Be careful, make the most of your own life first, don't do it too early.'

But she didn't actually TELL me in so many words what it would mean: that I wouldn't have my own will, that I would have to be a selfless person for twenty-three hours out of twenty-four, that my whole sense of self would be shaken. I felt conned and quite angry.

Freedom to be ourselves is something – like good health – that it's hard to appreciate the full value of until we lose it.

Harder still, perhaps, to explain what this loss of freedom means to a woman whose entire energies are devoted to preparing for the arrival of a new life:

The sense of outrage when it dawns on you what it means to be a mother! Why didn't anyone TELL me? Yet I don't see how anyone could communicate what it is about motherhood. If you do want a child you just shut off your mind to the things people say.

Then there are the things you *think* you are prepared for – like losing sleep. The intellectual acceptance of the fact that you are going to be tired is quite a different kettle of fish from the experience some women have of wakeful, broken nights for years on end. After all, sleep deprivation is known to be a form of torture which breaks down the strongest individuals.

Experiences like these rub off on how a mother feels towards a child. One of the more damaging consequences of the idealization of motherhood is that all mothers are expected – and often expect of themselves – to love their children unconditionally and always.

Yet love in its complexity encompasses strong and conflicting emotions. Mothers also feel anger, resentment, even hate towards their children at times. Some women end up with a dislike of their offspring. For many mothers, pulled in conflicting directions by their feelings, torn by their own needs versus their children's needs, motherhood becomes a state of being divided in the self.

There can be few mothers who have not at some time felt the urge to lash out at their children – despite the intense love they may feel for them at other times. The most devoted of mothers admit that they have felt like battering their babies at some point – and that they can't understand why it doesn't happen more often.

The poet Adrienne Rich writes about the case of an American mother who decapitated her two children on her suburban front lawn. She discusses it with a group of friends, who all have children. Not one displays the expected 'shock' reaction. All can identify with the action of the murderous mother. All have been that mother in imagination at least.

Be prepared?

Yet women spend their whole pregnancies preparing for their babies, don't they? For the *birth* of their babies, yes. Not for life after the birth. As far as the health service is concerned, being prepared means being fit and ready to push the baby out into the world.

But the influence the medical professionals can exert on a mother in pregnancy (because 'it's best for the baby') is in stark contrast to the absence of provision for her once she gets home. The birth process may have been taken out of her hands entirely and regulated by doctors with sophisticated equipment – all in the interests of delivering a healthy baby.

Yet should she take that healthy baby home and find herself in the grip of a fear that she may inflict hurt upon it – as often happens to depressed mothers – there is unlikely to be a soul in sight to help her. From the full care and control of the hospital, the mother is suddenly jettisoned into one hundred per cent individual responsibility for her baby. The only professional helper a new mother has to ease her way across the divide between hospital and home is her overworked health visitor, and there are precious few of these around.

Yes, the day of a baby's birth is vital, but every day following that for a long time to come is also important. It is considered irresponsible of women not to attend at least some ante-natal classes, preferably with their male partners in tow, but there are few post-natal classes. Meanwhile, 'parent-craft' classes remain woefully inadequate – where they exist at all.

When a teacher friend of mine tried to instruct her sixteen-year-old class about childcare, parents complained. Perhaps it's hard for parents to countenance their own childrens' possible parenthood because this entails acknowledging their sexuality, but such gaps in our education do nothing to help women through the 'appalling vacuum' of new motherhood.

It's often assumed that women don't need any education in bringing up children because we have a 'maternal instinct'. Yet we aren't expected to give birth without any help or instruction, and nor do we know automatically how to perform that most 'natural' of functions, breastfeeding.

Mothering is learned behaviour – learned usually from one's own mother. (Ann Oakley cites evidence to show that monkeys living in zoos do not know how to give birth, or to suckle their own babies.) Lack of adequate mothering may be responsible for setting up the cycle of child abuse: a woman feels that her own mother never met her needs and looks to her baby to meet those needs for love. When the baby cries – as all babies do – she feels a rejection which mirrors her own mother's lack of love for her, and reacts by punishing the baby.

Even thirty years ago a study in the *Lancet* showed that mothers believed they lacked some innate instinct and that they felt guilty and distressed by their shortcomings. It's a message that our society never registered, for now in the 1980s national organizations such as the Parent Network are being set up to help parents learn more about raising their families.

The Network aims to establish parent support groups to help them find new ways to communicate and improve their relationships with their children. They say that education for family life is patchy, that parents need information and help at every stage of their job, from their childrens' birth until they leave home. Parents today are often struggling in isolation and without guidance, says the Network, so that when things go wrong at home they are left feeling like dreadful failures.

Not only is there a dearth of education for motherhood, but the sheer invisibility of mothers' needs reinforces women's false expectations of the role. There is nothing to indicate to a childless woman as she walks down her local high street that the friendly shops, banks, libraries and offices could be a frustrating obstacle course for her once she is a mother.

If there were a mother and baby room at the public lavatory, she might realize that you can't take small babies and children out for long without having to feed and change them. If there were lifts in libraries and public buildings or pram parks outside shops she might register the thought that baby buggies make many places into no-go areas for mothers. If there were more family rooms in pubs she would see that mothers don't get to go out on their own very often. If there were a special mothers' till at the supermarket, women would see that even going shopping has its problems when you've got children. If there were a workplace nursery at the office she would be aware that children don't pass into suspended animation for the span of their parents' earning hours.

Little wonder that some women think there is a conspiracy of silence. The lack of provision for mothers allows people to go on thinking that mothers don't need special help or support, that motherhood is just a natural part of life that fits in easily with the way we already live. Until this situation changes too, the realities of the role will go on hitting women with shock.

No mother is an island

There is another change that children bring but which is so unpredictable that no woman can prepare for it: that is the change in her relationship with the baby's father. Many a woman experiences this as a divide within herself, for whereas she was once his wife or lover, she is now also someone else's mother – and there is a certain tension between the two roles.

If pregnancy seems a prelude quite out of tune with the subsequent song and dance, romantic courtship is even more at odds with the business of birth and motherhood. Who knows why people fall in love, but if it is all in aid of reproducing the race, nature plays a mean trick.

Perhaps he loves her for the freedom of her spirit, for the beauty of her body? How ironic then that the product of his love – their child – should so deeply jeopardize her autonomy and change her body irrevocably. He thought he had secured

64

first place in her affections, only to be usurped by a tiny tyrant whom he cannot fight. Now he lies in bed beside his woman, watching his baby suck on the breasts that he thought of as his preserve.

Some men can cope with these changes and develop a new and richer love for their partner. Some men can't, and a baby, far from cementing a relationship, can put it under breaking strain. But however their relationship changes, change it most irrevocably does, as a world of two people expands to become a world of three or four or more.

It can seem particularly hard on a new mother when such profound events are transforming her life and her relationship that she no longer has enough time to spend with the baby's father to talk about those changes. Women who get pregnant quite soon after they fall in love or get married say they feel a sense of regret that they have not had more time to be a twosome. Even when the child is very much wanted a woman can feel a conflict between her role as lover and her role as mother:

The only resentment that I felt about having my baby was that I was not able to be a wife to my husband any more. We didn't have time to be together, to go out, or even just to talk.

Sex too may be under seige from the new inhabitants of the home. There can't be many mothers around who don't have a tale to tell about a little figure toddling into the bedroom at a crucial moment. 'Mummy, are you out of breath? Are you puffed out, Mummy?', asked one such little coital interrupter of his rueful parent. And another little boy, very seriously, when noticed standing in the doorway: 'Mummy, I've been WONDERING what you are doing.'

Mother to mother

The arrival of a child brings into a different focus that other

65

most crucial relationship with the new mother's own mother. Isn't the grandmother ideally placed to tell her daughter what to expect from motherhood, how to adjust to its metamorphoses, how to deal with its divides? Isn't this an occasion which can bring the two closer together, give them a chance to share their most profound experiences?

Sometimes, in some cases, yes. A mother's own mother can be an invaluable source of support and information as well as a major emotional ally in a time of stress and change. But quite aside from the personal conflicts which do exist in every mother-daughter relationship, a generation is a long time and many things have changed since our own mothers first gave birth. As a result many of today's mothers feel they are under attack for not doing things 'properly' – i.e. the way their own mothers used to do them. Inevitably our own mothers compare our style of mothering with their own and – when they see us doing things differently – this seems like a rejection of the way they did it, a retrospective criticism of their own significant role.

Many women would like to turn to their own mothers for support, but even when these grandmothers are living nearby, their support is not always unqualified. As this woman puts it:

My mother was incredibly supportive to me (although she lives miles away), but underneath was the suggestion that she'd gone through it and survived, and so I would too, eventually.

Ann Dally writes in *Inventing Motherhood* that she has treated hundreds of women for feelings of depression and inadequacy as mothers and that criticism from their own mothers and mothers-in-law were a big part of their problems. These grandmothers would say to their daughters, 'If you can't look after your own children, you shouldn't have had them,' plunging the new mothers deeper into despair.

When Dally looked further into some of these cases she found that the older women had raised their own families with a lot of help from neighbours, relatives, even nannies. By contrast, their daughters were bringing up babies in isolation. Yet so completely had both generations of women absorbed the current thinking that babies need their mothers exclusively, that they couldn't see how much motherhood has changed. Rather than comparing notes with mothers of an earlier generation, it would seem more helpful to share the difficulties of motherhood with one's contemporaries. After all, mothers' difficulties often flow from contemporary situations and attitudes.

Women's desperate need for some way to bridge the gap between their former lives and their lives as mothers is reflected in a new trend in the National Childbirth Trust. One of their fastest growing sections is that of the post-natal support groups. 'Our members tell us that it keeps them sane to go to the groups,' says Hannah Corbishley of the NCT. 'They say they would be climbing the walls otherwise'.

The groups are run entirely by untrained women giving mother-to-mother support. These women are often people who have enjoyed being out at work, taking part in a social network, sharing jokes and ideas with colleagues. Then, says the NCT, they suddenly find themselves at home with a small baby. There's no one to talk to; the baby won't understand the jokes – it's a huge gap in the life of the new mother when she was expecting satisfaction and fulfilment.

Understandably, when women emerge from such a difficult period, many would rather forget all about it. As this mother puts it:

Once we've done our time – which adds up to about six years on average – we can put away the wheels and the nappies and feeding schedules. Then the enormous relief and rediscovery of freedom nearly forgotten makes us say, 'Well, its not long really and you soon forget.' Like the pain of labour really!

Of course, the good memories remain – memories of the joy, satisfaction and love which grow between mother and child. But it's a tragedy that women should also have such bleak memories of much of early childrearing that they want to obliterate what happened.

There's no doubt that many of these bad times are caused by our society's attitude to motherhood, as mothers find themselves caught in the gap between idealized motherhood and the totally undervalued reality. Psychologically, the higher a woman's expectations in life are, the more she seems to suffer, as this self-proclaimed middle-class mother has found:

Mothers lack status and that makes me angry and sad. The strange thing is that it is middle-class mothers who seem to lack status most of all. One has a break in one's career to have children: is that all the children are worth? A 'break'?

Conversely, the fact that we have to make this 'break' means that we expect a great deal from this experience and so we try to achieve the impossible with perfect births, perfect babies and, of course, perfectly contented mothers.

Old wives' tales

Conspiracy or not, there is no doubt that living in a man's world where birth is a medical matter has made it hard for women to keep dominion over this exclusively female experience.

From the time pregnancy is confirmed by a medical expert (the evidence of our own bodies is not enough), many women still complain that they are only the object, not the subject involved in childbearing. Producing a healthy baby becomes the doctor's job, not the mother's. Her version of what is happening to her often sinks into silence.

In our culture, the 'real' things in life, the things that matter, are male-defined, and men have no first-hand experience of motherhood. Women's experience tends to be obscured and made invisible even to ourselves. We cannot fully comprehend, let alone communicate, our own experience until we have built up our own truthful picture.

One of the bestselling books on the motherhood market in

recent years has been *Pregnancy* by Gordon Bourne (FRSC, FRCOG). His book, written from years of experience as a doctor and no doubt with the most helpful intentions, quite unselfconsciously reveals how prevailing male attitudes towards women are part and parcel of the way we deal with childbirth and of the false expectations which surround motherhood.

Not only does he argue that giving birth is the highest pinnacle of achievement for nature's finest specimens of womanhood (nature ensures that only the finest reproduce by making the poor, less 'feminine' specimens into lesbians!), but he also depicts women as passive and irrational creatures who need male guidance and protection. Hormonal changes in pregnancy make women 'emotionally unstable', writes Bourne, who in his book values the rational far above the emotional and intuitive:

Even the most highly competent and efficient woman may find that her judgement is impaired. She may be inclined to make hasty decisions, her reasoning may not be as rational as it would normally be and her conclusions may be inaccurate and incorrect.

In this state, Bourne warns his readers, the mother-to-be is specially vulnerable to:

unthinking friends and relations [who] may well regale her with unpleasant or even horrifying stories of their own experiences . . . Most of her fears will be absolutely groundless, but it is very difficult for a woman so far advanced in pregnancy and feeling so intimately involved with the symptoms to differentiate truth from fiction.

But Bourne reserves his strongest invective for those women who spread gloom and despondency with their 'old wives' tales':

Probably more is done by wicked women with their malicious lying tongues to harm the confidence and happiness of pregnant women than by any other single factor.

Why do they do this? Perhaps it is some form of sadism or as a revenge payment for an unhappy experience of their own that they wish to magnify and share with someone who cannot answer back.

The antidote to this barrage of feminine untruth, says Bourne, is the 'stabilizing influence' of the husband and the wisdom of the doctor. Thus a man who has never, who never will, give birth to a child, closes his ears to those who have – and recommends that other women do so too. No doubt he means well, and no doubt some women do make the most of their moments of drama (there's got to be some compensation!).

But if the fears, anxieties and stresses of childbearing are unhealthy imaginings of the hormone-befuddled female brain, it follows that the difficult and stressful aspects of motherhood aren't to be countenanced either.

Ideal milk of motherhood

A further powerful mechanism at work to prevent women from knowing what is in store for them is the idealization of motherhood. Mothers today know from their experience that, as an institution, motherhood is in a parlous state. For arguably the first time in history, women are expected to bring up children in almost total isolation, in a hostile environment and without real support. Mothers are exploited by the state, and by many individual men as a source of cheap labour. Mothers' work goes unrecognized, undervalued and unpaid. Yet at the same time motherhood is sold to us as the ultimate achievement for a woman.

We live in a society which organizes itself without consideration for the needs of children and their mothers. We face enormous problems as to who is to care for our children at a time when more than forty percent of the paid workforce is female. These are the realities behind the ideology which encourages the image of the wondrous Supermum, ever-caring, ever-sharing, taking the strain, sacrificing herself to care for her family – as it's only 'natural' she should.

Idealization is dangerous because it creates false expectations. It creates a divide which keeps women from realistic knowledge of motherhood and so leads to disillusion in new mothers. As a psychiatrist, Ann Dally sees such disillusion as catastrophic to women:

At present we are confronted by an epidemic of depression in women, most of them mothers. Many convert their depression into physical symptoms and are often treated by their doctors as though the cause of their troubles was ulcers, colitis or hormonal imbalance. Many make suicidal gestures as acts of despair or as desperate bids for attention – now the commonest cause of emergency admission to hospital.

From selective deafness to the breakdown in community, from the medical control of childbearing to the phoney state-sponsored image of motherhood, women have many obstacles to overcome before we narrow the gap between life BC (Before Children) and life AD (After Delivery).

It is going to take a great change in public consciousness and some drastic political rethinking, but the health and happiness of millions of women – and their children – depends upon it.

Me, myself, I

After their children are born, women have to adjust not only to the gap between their expectations and the reality of motherhood, but also to an enormous change in their perceptions of themselves. Having spent the first twenty, thirty or more years of her life in establishing her individual identity, the new mother finds that that identity has radically changed.

She has lost her autonomy. True, she may have already decided to share her life in marriage. But as our soaring divorce rate shows, women can and do leave their men. Yet most mothers feel they can't and won't leave their babies.

71

A new baby is still partly merged with its mother. When (or if) the mother sleeps it is with one ear open and she wakes when the baby stirs. When the baby cries, her breast milk spurts involuntarily. If the child is parted from her she may be anxious, even tearful. For at least the early months the baby's existence is inextricably linked to hers – she is no longer one person. Some women enjoy this dichotomy; others find it quite painful, but all know they are not the person they once were.

It's an awareness that is most intense for as long as a woman's children are small:

I went through an awful period of feeling that I had lost my identity. For a long time I felt I was becoming like my own mother, living her life, and she was someone who resented having children. It has taken me about two years to feel strong again. That's partly because the children are growing up, and now I'm ME again.

Eventually a mother's world returns to a semblance of what it was before, but she knows that her inner self has changed irrevocably:

I now feel as if I'm coming out of a childbearing bubble which has completely dominated my life for four years. I'm returning to the person I was before. For four years it has been totally emotionally and intellectually demanding, having these little people, wanting the next little person. Now I'm more in touch with the person I was and all sorts of other things are starting to fire my imagination. But there will always be a divide of a kind, as there will always be the difference between myself now that I have children and myself beforehand.

For women who grew up in the aftermath of the '60s and '70s, the desire for independence and autonomy is often a strong one. But the wish for children is also very powerful. So that even when women consciously 'choose' to become mothers, may feel a deep ambivalence about their new role, as this mother of two admits:

I spent years undoing the past, rejecting the conditioned female role.

72

I felt I had just got to the point where I was free to do what I wanted without having to trouble about anyone else. I had just found myself. To throw all that away in having children seemed crazy, and yet I did it. I can't explain that.

Many mothers, for as long as circumstances make it necessary, do submerge their own desires for freedom. But that's not because it comes 'naturally', but usually because we've got no choice. No matter how much a woman wants her children, the frustration she feels at being so powerless and trapped can be a source of great internal conflict and guilt.

Today's woman is used to making her decisions about her own life. She is used to having control over her income, her home, her job, her choice of relationships. She has probably chosen to be a mother too, but much as she might love her baby, on another level the child becomes the cuckoo which takes over her own nest, ousting her former free self:

This is the first time in my life that I have not been able to make decisions for myself. It's not just ME any more: the family is a parcel. I still make decisions but they are in the interests of the children – which might be against my own interests.

Sometimes the loss of a woman's physical freedom – as when she can't escape her breastfeeding or sleeping child – becomes the symbol of a more general rage she feels over the loss of selfhood. This mother has an instance engraved in her memory from a time when her baby was four months old:

I was at the sink, washing nappies – again – while the baby was asleep. My husband was in the garden chopping wood, then going shopping – just doing boring weekend jobs, but jobs that we used to do together. And I was thinking 'There he goes AGAIN! He's gone off somewhere!'. I felt absolutely trapped, stuck at home.

The constant demands of children for physical contact – demands to be held, picked up, cuddled, sat on one's lap – can at times be irritatingly claustrophobic. After months of breastfeeding my child – which I did gladly – I used to feel an alarming sense of repulsion as she clasped hold of me for yet another feed. I was so fed up with not being able to put her down, with having to sit or lie still while she fed that I had to control an urge to push her away.

Perhaps it's a natural feeling at the time for weaning: we've all seen animals nip or shove at their young when they're getting too big for suckling yet still nuzzling for their mother's nipple. But being human, I felt a bit guilty that I wanted my body back for myself – to be able to run, to go swimming, to feel physically free. Yet when my baby was not in my arms I also felt a hollow lack and missed her.

Someone else's body, someone else's life

For one of the facts of a woman's new existence that may take her by surprise is the change in her physical self, and the change in other people's reaction to that self. 'Normality' as our society perceives it is to be fit, firm, free and definitely not fecund. Most women do enjoy a time when they are proud and confident in their bodies before they give birth.

But as her belly swells in pregnancy, the mother-to-be begins to deviate from that norm. It may be a welcome relief, but she notices that men pay her less attention, or at least attention of a different, non-sexual kind. If they flirted with her previously they were unlikely publicly to touch her. But now they reach out their hands without a qualm to feel her belly. The boundaries of her body have changed in more ways than one.

After she gives birth it seems for a while as if her body will never return to 'normal'. She leaks and she bleeds. She can't do up her jeans around her flabby tummy. Her breasts have grown into someone else's (literally), and unless she wears pads, little circles of milk keep staining the front of her jumper. Having heard the kind of 'jokes' that men make about women with 'enormous' vaginas, she may even wonder whether her body is still sexually attractive to men. Of course, it's only a matter of time before she does have her fitness back and her body is more like its old self. But she – and usually her man – have seen it through such an extraordinary transformation that neither can think of it in quite the same way again.

The change in a mother's day-to-day work also brings a change of image which divides her from her former self. As a student I did a lot of travelling, and have a cameo engraved on my memory from that time. I was on a train, travelling alone, with only a rucksack and perfect freedom to go where I liked when I liked. Across the train corridor I watched a young mum struggling to keep her baby happy during the journey. She seemed infinitely weighted down with bags and parcels and tissues and trolleys and I pitied her from the bottom of my heart.

But sooner or later all mothers find themselves in the role that once they pitied which makes it quite hard not to feel sorry for oneself. However helpful her man, however determined she is not to become a household drudge, many a mother ends up doing a great deal more housework, cooking and cleaning than she did in her previous child-free incarnation. We may fight not to see ourselves as the stereotype of a skivvy, so it comes as a shock when we see just that image reflected back to us from our own children – as happened to this mother of two:

My son was in the garden with his father, when I turned to go inside with my little girl. She said, 'Yes, that's right, Mummy, the girls go back into the house.'

Or, as her toddler son told his mother as she appeared in the garden:

Get back in the kitchen, Mummy!

Such innocent remarks can bring mothers up short against the knowledge that – if only temporarily – they have changed into the 'housewife' which they never wanted to be.

75

New autonomy?

The ways in which mothers deal with their loss of autonomy are as many and varied as women themselves. Some fight it; some accept it; some even relish it.

For some women the loss of freedom to motherhood can be an excuse not to compete. One mother told me how she felt terror at the impending departure of her last teenager. She was an artist, and for years had had no time to work full stretch. Now she fears, without the buffer of her children, she will be revealed as lacking in talent. Even if no one else expects it, she no longer has the excuse she made for herself not to go all out.

Alternatively, lack of freedom can feel like security. In the words of the song, 'Freedom's just another word for nothing left to lose . . . for nothing left to do.' Before the Pill and before the latest wave of feminism, women had fewer choices. Some say they were glad to know just what their role was. It suited some women to believe that motherhood should be their sole commitment.

Today's mother has more choices – well and good. But with that she has more dilemmas. She rarely accepts that her identity should be completely submerged in that of her children. With our smaller families, the childrearing years are fewer than they were, and she will probably have years ahead of her to carry on with her own life as her children grow towards independence.

But how does she – or does she ever – regain her sense of self after motherhood? Some women look back on the person they were before motherhood and simply can't believe that they were ever that confident in dealing with the outside world. Years of spending most of one's time with small children and years of being treated as 'just a housewife' (as happens to women who take a 'break' from paid work) leave many mothers feeling that they aren't capable of doing anything else. A friend, who held down an extremely demanding professional job for years before her children were born, now tells me she feels it was 'all a con'.

There is even a sense – which comes with the overwhelming commitment of the early years – that motherhood is 'it'. But as this mother was reminded by some older women friends, mothers have to grow out of the early motherhood identity as surely as their children have to grow up:

Losing your confidence after having children is a major thing a lot of women go through and have to knock on the head. It takes a lot of work. I'm very grateful to the friends who said to me, 'Come on, think about yourself and what you are going to do in the forty or fifty years after you have two tiny tots.' It's a battle to see yourself in a different role, where you are and where you can go, which directions you can develop – when there are a lot of conflicting pressures to deal with.

For many mothers it's a life of compromises, multiple adjustments – and not a little guilt:

Your autonomy is lost. But you have to make yourself a new autonomy or you don't survive . . . You do this by juggling your needs with those of your kids, juggling for the rest of your life.

A 'working' mother?

Perhaps the most stressful juggling act of all for today's mothers comes when they go back to paid work. Having thrown themselves so completely into the gear for motherhood, it can feel like a wrenching reverse to take on the employee identity again – which fits so badly with the role of mother.

Today's mothers often feel guilty if they go back to work, yet most of them have no choice. Just as the nation's economy depends on women's work, so many households depend on women having an income. A quarter of mothers go back to paid work before their first child's first birthday. By the time their youngest is ten, some three quarters of all mothers are in paid employment, although most of these are working part-time – presumably because of their family commitments.

This generation of mothers grew up in the wave of reaction against the 50's stereotype of housewifely contentment. Women fought for the right to work, for the right to seek fulfilment, satisfaction, independence and status through their jobs. The return of married women to the job market has been one of the great social changes of our times.

For some women this has been a great boon:

I don't think I'm cut out to be a full time mum, and to be able to go to work during the day, and to have my daughter in the evenings and on weekends is for me the best of both worlds. I'm fortunate to have a nanny whom I trust and whom my little girl loves. And I think I'm a happier, more enthusiastic mother for the fact that I do have time off from mothering during the week.

But returning to paid work has not always been a change for the better. For some women it has not even been a change – like the working class women who always have worked but in low paid, low status jobs without security or long term benefits. Many of them would rather have the right NOT to work, but instead the right to stay at home to bring up their children.

And whatever their class, there is grief and guilt and sadness at being parted from one's children for so much of the day. As a freelance writer, I am far more fortunate than most mothers in being able to organize my own working hours to fit in with childcare. I arranged to take up work again gradually, when my baby was about five months old.

It seemed an ideal set up: Marie the childminder lived just across the street and she sent her children over to tell me if my baby was crying or needed to be breastfed. Maeve was only there for a few hours a week. But still I found the separation hard, and reacted to every phone call or knock at the door as if it were bound to be a signal that Maeve was in distress.

One day I left her at her minder's house and walked on to the post office. A few minutes later, Marie turned up with Maeve in her buggy, a few places behind me in the queue. I was mortified and upset beyond all rational explanation. There was MY baby with another woman!

I had to greet Marie while making sure Maeve didn't see me, and then stand there in that interminable queue. Of course she did see me and did cry, and I had to leave the Post Office before I had bought any stamps, unable to bear it.

Now Maeve has been at the same childminder's house, Heather's, for over a year. Heather says they think of her as part of the family, and when Maeve comes home she talks about Heather and her children and about what they have been doing all day.

This arrangement is such a happy one that sometimes when I drop Maeve off in the mornings I can't imagine why I'm leaving the company of children playing and having fun to go back to my lonely word processor in its empty office.

And there are a few emotional trip wires for mothers when children become very fond of their carers – as ideally they should be. Of course I want Maeve to love to be at Heather's, but I'm not sure how I feel when she decides (as she has on occasion) that she's having such good games there that she doesn't want to be taken home!

A friend told me rather ruefully about her toddler who also spends the week with a childminder who he loves, called 'Auntie' in the family. One Saturday the little boy romped into his parents' room, jumped on the bed and asked 'when can I go to Auntie's please?'. She too is delighted that her little boy is happy with his minder, less sure how this reflects on her.

Here is a dilemma which is at the heart of a working mother's life. She wants, usually with the child's father, to be the most important person in the child's young life. But can she really expect to be so if the child is spending most of the time with someone else?

We reassure ourselves that it is quality and not quantity of time that counts, that mother-love starts earlier, goes deeper and lasts longer than anyone else's. But if we suspect in our hearts that our small children would rather be in their mothers' company, then we also suspect that a price is being paid for our freedom to work. Already, many mothers are themselves paying some of that price in psychological suffering.

Every working mother asks herself whether she is doing the right thing – right by herself and right by the children. Work may bring her self-fulfilment, money and the chance to build a better material future for her children.

But can those benefits be weighed up against the closeness of the mother-child relationship? Is there any substitute for the invaluable emotional security that can come to children for having a mother always at home?

Some of us believe that we would not have better relationships with our children if we spent all day at home with them. A woman who resents being 'stuck at home' will somehow pass that resentment on to her children. Some of us are quite relieved to have no choice: many married women as well as single parents rely on their own income.

Is it in the nature of motherhood itself to require a sacrifice from women – or is our society at fault for making the options so awkward? It's certainly true that social changes could, and in some countries have, taken a huge amount of stress off the shoulders of working mothers by providing decent parental leave and childcare.

But time and again these questions come back to haunt us. They have no simple answers when children are small, and by all accounts, they don't go away as children grow older.

The teen trap

Mothers of young children look forward, sometimes desperately, to the time when their children are old enough to have some degree of independence. What bliss to have children that don't have to be spoon fed but who can cook a meal for themselves. What bliss to have children who can take care of their own clothes and cleanliness. How marvellous to have children who don't demand every bit of your presence whenever they can get it.

80

But according to mothers of teenage children, it doesn't get easier to be a working mother as children grow older – it gets harder. By the time children are in their teens, many mothers have reached a crucial stage in their careers. Achievement at work has brought more pressure and more responsibility. But just about the same time, children have got to the point of making new demands on their mothers – and demands on their own terms.

There was a time when a hard-pressed mother could put her children to bed in the course of the evening and have at least a few hours for herself or her partner. But teenage children won't go to bed at seven or eight. They want to watch the telly, or talk, or they need help with their homework.

Mothers of older children may not have to worry about nappies and colic any longer, but they do have the dread of their child's involvement with drugs to keep them awake at night – and the minefields of sex to negotiate.

Toddler tantrums give way not to perfect peace, but to teenage traumas. 'No' doesn't necessarily mean 'no' any more, not when a youngster has decided to rebel against and challenge and reject every parental dictate.

There's no need to stay at home any more if nannies or babies are sick, but the working mother's back-up system of housekeeper or au pair is not infallible either.

As children grow older they seem to need their mothers not less, but differently. Maire Messenger Davies is a psychologist with two teenaged children and she told *Good Housekeeping* how her fourteen-year-old daughter Hannah keeps tabs on her:

It's rather strange that Hannah, who in principle is quite a feminist, should still repeat that the best moment of her day is when she turns down the garden path after school and sees me standing at the kitchen sink.

Even when children have technically left home, their apparent independence can mask a great vulnerability and need for parental back-up at times. As this mother of university students told *Good Housekeeping*:

Two of my daughters are at university now but when they come home they protest if I go out in the evening. 'Oh WHEN will you be back?' they say, 'Must you really go?'.

But then perhaps, we all, in some deep ways, always need our mothers. And there are compensations in being needed.

Pushmepullyou

Unfortunately, the right to carry on in paid work after having children (nebulous as it is) hasn't brought women the right to relax when they get home. Instead they are caught in the trap of the double shift, competing with men on male ground at work while still carrying the burden of domestic work and childcare at the end of the office day.

The strain has been immense, and to some extent women have helped to heap the coals on their own heads by endorsing the myth of the Superwoman. How many women have been driven to – or over the edge – of breakdown in emulation of this ideal? If it weren't for the understandable desire to take up new opportunities and prove ourselves in the world of work, women might have been more alert to the fact that they were being turned into 24-hour, schizophrenic work-horses.

After all, if this is such an enviable ideal why don't we see our magazines and newspapers full of articles about the wonderful MEN who get up at dawn to see the kids off to school, put in a hard day at the boardroom and then nip off home to create gourmet treats for the missus in an immaculate house? Because most men would be aghast at having to work that hard, that's why.

Mothers are pulled in one direction by their jobs, pushed in another by their families. In the extreme division between home and the workplace which characterizes our post-industrial society, there are virtually no allowances made for women's dual role – and even less for male employees' roles as fathers.

This leaves mothers in a condition of constant division. As Harriet Harman, the Labour MP for Peckham and mother of three puts it, 'its a state of feeling constantly torn in two.' She has many friends who also combine motherhood with careers, and who call themselves 'closet mothers'. At work they have to pretend they don't have any children – or face disapproval from their bosses.

I've worked in an office where several married women would regularly make a phone call at about four o'clock in the afternoon. With voices lowered they would whisper what sounded like endearments and pet names into the telephone. At first I thought there might be affairs in the offing. Only later did it dawn on me that they were surreptitiously ringing childminders and nannies to make domestic arrangements – and having a few stolen moments of chat with the children.

It's hard enough to balance children and work when things are going well at home. But when a child is unhappy or ill, the working mother may find her juggling act becomes a desperate sleight of hand. A colleague who worked for a large publisher has told me that when her child was sick – or when the child's nanny was sick – she would ring her boss to say that she herself had the 'flu. She knew that her male boss simply wouldn't understand or accept the true situation.

Women bosses aren't necessarily more sympathetic. Indeed some of them seem to be worse. A senior social worker in Scotland – she has three children – also has to pretend to her (female) boss that she is ill whenever one of the children goes down with a bug. Later, being a conscientious worker, she rings back when she knows the boss will be out to tell her colleagues 'If you need to consult me please call me at home, I had to lie to the boss again.'

A colleague who has recently become a mother freely admits that she was quite unsympathetic at work towards women with children – until she had her own:

I used to think – Oh not another pregnancy, what a bloody bore!

Chris Gowdridge, Co-Ordinator of the charity Maternity Alliance, deplores the way that British employers behave towards parents. 'They treat maternity like a broken leg,' she says. 'The fact that while you're away you've produced a child is ignored. The attitude is 'you're back at work now, so its all going to be as before'.

By contrast, most European employers treat maternity as a manageable part of working life, like sick leave, delays in recruitment and time off for holidays. Britain is the only country in Europe that doesn't have some form of parental leave. Nine out of ten EEC countries provide fathers with some leave. In Britain, we don't allow them a single day.

But with children still seen as a woman's responsibility, it is Britain's mothers that are left with the heartache and headache of finding childcare for their children in order to go out to earn a living. A lot depends on where a woman lives, yet childcare in this country tends to be both scarce and expensive. Nor do the hours of nurseries and schools fit with those of the convention-al office or nine-to-five job.

As a result 'working mothers' (every mother is a working mother!) often feel they are doing two jobs, but neither of them properly. Pauline Jellicoe is a nurse and mother of two, and as she told *She* magazine, life since her divorce has meant strug-gling to survive with a series of low paid jobs for unsympathe-tic employers.

She worked nights, she worked part time, as a cleaner, a receptionist, a nurse, always trying to fit her hours around the needs of her children. While at work she was always worried about the children:

I had to leave before they went to school, so always I kept thinking: 'Have they remembered their bus fare? Have they put warm coats on? . . . and school holidays and weekends were always a problem . . . I feel so bad about not being around all the time . . . There are always things they forget to tell me, and you never seem to have conversations because you're always rushing.'

84

This is not so much a state of being divided as of being splintered. But the alternative for many women is a life on social security or without their own income. Women, as much as men, need and benefit from the identity and independence of paid work, and from the adult companionship of colleagues.

Even for women who do live with men, the strain is not necessarily less. Men rarely do their fair share of the housework and childcare, as Helen Lentell has confirmed in researching a BBC programme on 'working mothers'. She found that whatever the class or working set-up of the family, even when men were unemployed, women were still coming home from paid work to take the responsibility for the house and for childcare.

When men do 'help' (i.e. it's not really their job) they tend to do the positive, fun things like playing and reading stories while the women do the washing and changing and cooking. Yet women still say they feel grateful for even a little help from their husbands.

Until 'help' becomes sharing, until men take on and acknowledge the value of such work, mothers have a battle on their hands. For man-made motherhood is not constructed with women's interests at heart.

PART TWO

MAN-MADE
MOTHERHOOD

CHAPTER 4

Rock the cradle, rock the boat

Oh mother, oh dear . . .

Over the door of the 'ladies' ' in my local pub hangs these verses, inscribed in elaborate olde worlde italics:

Mother

God made many lovely things
Sunset and flowers and trees
Birds and starlight and loyal friends
And after He made all these

He gave another gift more rare
More loving and more true
A wonderful person most fair
A mother dear as you.

As I sup my pint I contemplate these sentiments and realize with some surprise that perhaps they are meant to refer to me. But if they are, I'm not supposed to be reading them. For I'm supposed to be at home with my child as He who made me so fair and rare didn't think to reward me by making it possible to go to that adult place of communion, the pub, in the company of the one who reveres me so, my child.

The people who *are* meant to be reading these verses are the men who relax at the bar while mother is at home getting dinner ready. How reassuring for them to know that she is doing so, not because she's got no choice because they have gone to the pub, but because He created her such a wonderful loving and true person.

So what the verses really mean is this:

Man made many useful things
Empires, the Bomb and such
Which save him from toil and gather him cash
Yet in order to make so much

He extended his power in order to keep
Women docile and easy to run
He created the ideal of Motherhood
It's 'natural' and it's cheap.

The raising of motherhood on to a pedestal is a propaganda tactic essential to a system which relies on women's exploitation. On one level it's a familiar form of manipulative flattery, used by people everywhere to do what they can't or won't do themselves: 'Darling, why don't you cook the dinner/sew my buttons/change that nappy; you're so much better at it than I am.'

It is powerful because it is (in part) what women want to hear, and it is what women know to be true in some respects at least. Motherhood *can* be wonderful, glorious, loving and fulfilling, and women crave recognition of their worth as mothers.

But the reason why the idealizing of motherhood is so damaging to women is because the praise rings hollow in the emptiness of any real support, status, or recognition for mothers. The more they tell us how wonderful we are, the more they expect us to carry on working without help and without complaint.

Putting motherhood on to a pedestal is a way of saying that nothing could be a more praiseworthy and fulfilling vocation for a woman. Would that it were so! But the ideal of motherhood becomes an impossible, intimidating standard when so many women are compelled by economic and political necessity to struggle against motherhood as drudgery.

At the same time as mother on her pedestal tells us how magnificent is motherhood, she also keeps us in our place by showing us how hopelessly inferior we are in our personal failure to live up to the ideal.

This gap between ideal and reality is at the root of many of the divisions which separate mothers from non-mothers, and of the conflicts within themselves which so many mothers experience.

Mother in myth

Mother on her pedestal is all-giving, all-caring. She is loving strength personified. The images of the Madonna, of Britannia the Motherland, even of good old mom and apple pie permeate our culture as paradigms of virtue and self-sacrifice.

We live in a secular age and tend to forget how much our culture has been shaped by religion. Yet for two thousand years the figure of the Virgin Mary has stood for quintessential feminine virtue. As Marina Warner points out in her book *Alone of All Her Sex*, the Christian mother of God is a symbol which exerts a powerful pull on our unconscious lives – and yet she is also clearly a product of male-dominated culture and history.

The Virgin, she argues, is central to Western attitudes to women as the embodiment of all that is traditionally thought of as feminine and appropriate to motherhood: she is soft, yielding, merciful, tolerant and receptive. But unlike Oriental culture, which expects to see masculine and feminine qualities, yin and yang, present and balanced in all individuals, Western thought has split the feminine characteristics from the masculine and has expected women to manifest only the feminine and men only the masculine.

To any girl brought up in the Catholic religion, the Virgin Mary is a powerful influence on her view of womanhood and motherhood – whether she accepts her example or rebels against it, as so many do. In alcoves all around my convent school her image stood, blue-robed, serene, looking down upon us in plaster compassion. Even on the way to netball matches we would be expected to kneel at her statue in the shrubbery and sing *Ave Maria*. Like any good mother, she would ask Father (God) to be lenient with us and help us come out on top. So, through religion's hierarchy, we were taught the way of the world – and just where we stood in the pecking order.

As a young girl, the image of the Virgin and my feelings about my mother were closely identified. In my eyes my mother – like the Virgin Mary – was a totally loving, calm and secure presence, patient and kind, a cool blue cloak of protection. Once, under anaesthetic gas at the dentist, I saw the Virgin Mary standing by me in her blue cloak, weeping for me as my tooth was pulled. When I came to, it was my mother standing there, myself making the crying sounds.

So strong is the influence of the Virgin on women's image of themselves that in the USA the word 'Marianismo' has been coined as a counterpart to male 'machismo' or 'macho' behaviour. Women in San Francisco of Latin American descent are known as 'Marian' when they behave in traditionally feminine ways – that is with passivity and self-denial, responding to the needs of their husbands and children with limitless patience, always putting their needs ahead of their own.

Implicit in the reverence paid to the mother of God is a deep insult to all other mothers, for she is revered for what we have lost – virginity. That Christ could only be born of a virgin speaks volumes of male disgust for women's sexual nature and the physical realities of motherhood. No matter how closely a woman may try to live up to the Virgin, she will still never be the equal of a man. For Christianity inherited the strong misogyny of both Judaism and of classical culture.

The Greeks taught that the man who led a good life might return to his native star: the man who didn't live a good life faced reincarnation as a woman. Aristotle is well known for his assertion of male superiority, classing women as inferiors – like slaves.

The stories of the Bible carry on the theme of women's innate inferiority, with man 'giving birth' to woman from his rib. Eve then gets them both cast out of Eden for her sins. The guilt and suffering of humanity are the result of woman's frailty, for which Christ died on the cross. The pains of labour, menstruation and the humiliation of producing milk from her breasts were seen as woman's special punishment for her evil. In Christian thinking, women must submit to the biological destiny which has been their curse since the Fall.

St Paul confirmed that women should remain as men's subordinate helpers, to be the glory of their husbands who were made in the image of God. Augustine and Aquinas could find no reason for the creation of woman, except for her role as childbearer: to them it seemed that in every other respect a man would have been a better helpmate to Adam.

But it was the Franciscans who completed the image of woman as humble worshipper of her child. According to Marina Warner, it was they who brought her down from her starry throne in heaven to depict her as meek, mild and tender, glorified in motherhood as she humbly prostrated herself before the Christ child. She quotes Simone de Beauvoir:

For the first time in human history the mother kneels before her son; she freely accepts her inferiority. This is the supreme masculine victory, consummated in the cult of the Virgin – it is the rehabilitation of woman through the accomplishment of her defeat.

A woman's lot?

Just as God was being pronounced dead in the modern age, science and psychoanalysis came to the rescue of mother on her pedestal. Darwin's theory of evolution helped confirm the Victorian view that while men were driven by strong sexual urges, women's instinct lay with motherhood. Men were supposed to be more highly evolved than women, in that they could control their sexual urges through exercising their superior capacity for will, while women were more primitive beings in that they never could escape the dictates of their biology. As Havelock Ellis wrote, 'Women's brains are in a sense . . . in their wombs.'

Middle-class women in Victorian times who showed themselves to have an inappropriate sexual appetite (it was considered normal for working-class women to be sexual) were sometimes 'treated' by the removal of the womb, ovaries or clitoris. Some kinds of strong emotion in women are still called 'hysteria' today, a word which derives from the Greek word for womb, and so the notion of women as ruled by their reproductive organs lives on.

Freudianism also stepped in to support the notion that true fulfilment for women lay in motherhood. As Lucy Bland points out in *Sex and Love*, women were supposed to reach sexual maturity with the move from the clitoris to the vagina as the true seat of pleasure. Lesbians were thought to be 'stuck' in an immature phase and still overly attached to their mothers.

Then in the wake of two world wars came the 1950s, a time of enormous emphasis on mothering. As Lucy Bland writes:

It became almost impossible to imagine women not wanting to be wives and mothers since this was the area in which they could really 'find' and fulfil themselves.

Perhaps for the first time in our history the emphasis was on a kind of mothering which demanded the full-time and exclusive care of the biological mother. The writings of John Bowlby, who studied children in institutions who were orphaned or separated from their families, focused on the vital importance of 'mother love' to children.

Much of what he wrote, however, was widely generalized to apply to all mothers and all children, without examining too closely what mother love might mean – how some mothers have got more love to give than others, how cash and circumstances and family problems can affect mother-child relationships, how some mothers can be better mothers for *not* spending twenty-four hours a day at home. The fear of 'maternal deprivation' with its ghastly consequences for children became a new curfew for women.

It was no accident that this new style of mothering coincided with the return of Britain's menfolk from the second world war. While they had been in the armed forces, the women had worked to keep the nation and its industries going and state-run nurseries took care of the children. But as the men came home and wanted their jobs back, the nurseries were closed and the women packed off to domestic life again. Bowlby's theories were used to prove how much children needed the unstinting attention of mother, and mother alone.

It is only by looking into the history of motherhood – not something girls are taught in school – that it becomes clear how mother on her pedestal is a man-made artefact, moulded and remoulded to show women how they should behave. All of us to some extent are the creatures of the culture we live in, and it's hard not to absorb these values even when they are not in our best interests.

It remains one of the great 'givens' of our society that women are born to be mothers. So widespread is the assumption that it may be hard for a woman to feel that she is truly feminine – in the traditional sense – until she conceives.

Adrienne Rich (in her personal exploration of motherhood *Of Woman Born*) recalls how she was merely *acting* the feminine role until pregnancy won her the social seal of approval as a real woman:

As soon as I was visibly and clearly pregnant I felt, for the first time in my adolescent and adult life, not guilty. The atmosphere of approval in which I was bathed – even by strangers on the streets it seemed – was like an aura I carried with me, in which doubts, fears, misgivings, met with absolute denial. 'THIS IS WHAT WOMEN HAVE ALWAYS DONE.'

Of course, many women do experience an extraordinarily powerful desire for children, for many intricate and complex reasons. But so strong is the external pressure upon women to become mothers that it takes a brave woman to admit she doesn't desire children. Whether she feels she wouldn't be any good at motherhood, or whether she wants to express her creativity in other ways, she risks being judged 'neurotic' and 'selfish'.

Idealized motherhood has not only – by contrast – made real motherhood far more painful for women, but it has relegated non-mothers to the realms of the 'unnatural' and 'barren'. From which position, who can blame them for looking somewhat askance at their sisters who seem to have fallen for the pro-motherhood propaganda?

Meanwhile the women who are mothers may well wonder if they will ever again have time or energy to topple the oppressive Ideal from her pedestal – to reveal what a divisive force she has been.

Not the nanny state

In the 1980s we are living in a time of strong ideological shoring up of mother on the pedestal. Thatcher's so-called Victorian values, Tebbit's attacks on the 'permissive' society, Conservative family policy – all are designed to reaffirm 'the family' instead of the state as the right place for taking care of people.

But when they say the family is the right place they mean it is the *cheaper* place for looking after people. As Ann Oakley puts it:

People are fond of saying that there is no more honourable profession (than motherhood) in modern society, yet it is one of the only two honourable professions which receive no financial recognition – the other one is housework. Clearly society has a tremendous stake in insisting on a woman's natural fitness for the career of mother: the alternatives are all too expensive.

96

And who more fitted to reflect society's ideas of 'natural fitness' than Britain's own Royal Family? Although the financial costs of parenthood aren't an issue in this family, the Royals have been most vigorously deployed to encourage the nation's womanhood into Motherhood.

How the media slavered over the perfections of Princess Diana! She may not be very brainy they hinted – but never mind, that's not important in a woman. What counts is that she worked with little children before she married Charles. Cut out to be a mother!

Diana's body became the terrain for a battle between two mutually incompatible images of feminine perfection – slimness and pregnancy. How the nation marvelled as she produced two male heirs and lost weight at the same time.

Princess Caroline of Monaco has also become a paradigm of motherly virtue – after a pretty shakey start. *Woman* magazine (September, 1986) shows her with her second husband and two children, under the title 'How I found happiness at last':

Tormented by her first marriage failure, devastated by her mother's death, Princess Caroline of Monaco might have broken down four years ago. Instead, she learned 'I could find the solution within myself.' Now happily remarried and a mother of two, she has found a new purpose.

Motherhood is held to be – quite literally – the solution within a woman's self, her happiness and her purpose. Which is why the press can't wait for Sarah Ferguson to join the throng by giving Prince Andrew an heir. The *Star*'s centre spread (21 July 1986) asked 'What sort of mum will Fergie make?', and answered itself with 'SMASHING!'

Fergie is not (yet) a mum, but nevertheless she is pictured holding someone else's baby. Much of the story is devoted to the notion that Fergie is bound to be a 'smashing' mum as she knows from bitter experience how awful it is to have a 'bad' one. Her own mother is described as having 'waltzed off with an Argentinian polo player.' No less an authority than Fergie's

mother's own mother is brought in to condemn this act of
unMotherly selfishness:

No one could understand how she could have left the children, it was
a frightful scandal.

Blaming the mother

Any woman who fails to live up to the impossible ideal of
motherhood is likely to be publicly scourged for her shocking
inadequacy. Blaming the mother is a national sport. When
Linda Gill and her four children were massacred in their
Redruth home in Cornwall in 1986 by her ex-policeman
husband Colin Gill, the papers blamed Linda. 'ALL DEAD'
screamed the *Star*'s headline, over a front page picture of the
whole family, 'BECAUSE THE MOTHER IN THIS PICTURE
FELL IN LOVE WITH THIS MAN' (above a snapshot of her
much younger lover). Surely, they were all dead because Colin
Gill couldn't control his jealousy and anger, and because he
shot them all?
   Even more unjust – for this mother lives on in guilt and pain
– was the treatment meted out to Gail Keating, whose three-
year-old daughter Leoni was abducted, sexually assaulted and
murdered by Gary Hopkins in September 1985.
   The press blamed Gail for leaving Leoni alone in the caravan, accusing her of putting her need to go drinking ahead of
her child's welfare. What they neglected to point out was that
Gail was taking her other daughter to a party which the older
child would have been disappointed to miss. Her babysitter
was late – Gail had never before left Leoni without a sitter –
and so Gail locked the caravan door and took her other
daughter to the party. There she was told by friends that the
sitter was back at the caravan, but in the twenty-minute gap
before her arrival, Leoni was abducted.
   Yet, again, it was the mother who was blamed for the
murder rather than the man who committed it. 'It wasn't me

who killed her. It wasn't my responsibility,' Gail was led to protest against the media chorus of condemnation. George Gale in the *Sunday Mirror* (29 June 1986) couldn't deny the obvious truth of that, yet he still found a way of blaming her.

Under the title SO LONELY LEONI he wrote:

But Gail Keating left three-year-old Leoni by herself in a caravan when she went out to a club. The killing may not have been Gail Keating's responsibility, but Leoni was.

These are extreme and tragic examples of an attitude which all mothers experience at one level or another. As one mother told me, 'When we bring up our children well, people say "Aren't you lucky to have such a lovely child!" But when the child does anything bad they say, "Where did the mother go wrong?"

Of course, women have been softened up all through their girlhood to accept the fact that we are guilty and blameworthy. So by the time we become mothers we're well used to being told we're doing everything wrong. If we don't breastfeed we're damaging the child, but if we breastfeed in public or for too long it's disgusting. If we don't discipline our children they'll grow up to be hooligans, but if we do discipline them we might stunt their development/ruin their self-esteem/ undermine their confidence.

If we love them not enough they will turn into psychopaths, but if we love them too much we will smother them or 'pervert' their sexuality. If we stay at home all day we'll be boring 'housewives' who deserve to lose our men to more alluring females, but if we go out to work we'll have families of 'latch-key' kids rampaging through the inner cities in an orgy of delinquency.

Mother-blaming is part and parcel of society's widespread denigration and undervaluing of women, and as such it finds a reflection in our language, our jokes and our general attitudes towards mothers. In her book *The Myth of Women's Masochism*, psychologist Dr Paula Caplan explores the idea that not

99

only are women supposed to be born to suffer (especially mothers in the pains of childbirth), but that they are also supposed to want and enjoy that suffering. She tells a classic 'Jewish mother' (read masochistic mother) 'joke':

Question: How many Jewish mothers does it take to change a light bulb?
Answer: None. 'It's alright, I'll sit in the dark . . .'

Caplan quotes a colleague's observations on American slang:

A nasty woman is a 'bitch', but a nasty man isn't nasty in his own right: he's a 'son of a bitch' or a 'bastard', both words reflecting badly on his mother.

Especially disturbing are the results of a study that Caplan made into the attitudes of mental health professionals towards mothers. After extensive research she found that – in spite of work in recent decades to change attitudes towards the roles of men and women – in the mental health field, it is as if the women's movement never happened.

Clinicians, reports Caplan, still overwhelmingly blame mothers for their children's problems – and blame the mothers of those mothers for *their* problems. In total contrast, her research found that the role of fathers in childrens' development is ignored or given tacit approval, even when it includes behaviour like heavy drinking or taking drugs in front of children.

Caplan argues that society is saying to women:

'We're offering you a job, but if anything goes wrong, even if it's forty or fifty years later, YOU will be held totally responsible for it.' If anyone offered you a job on those terms you'd tell them to keep it. But that is the position in which mothers are placed. It is no wonder that they often come to mothering filled with fear, guilt and anxiety. Then they are called masochistic for suffering in that role, and when they try to avoid causing problems for their children by meeting their children's needs and neglecting or denying their own, they are called masochistic for their self-neflect.

100

Surely one of the cruellest areas of mother-blaming is that of cot-deaths. All too often a mother who has just been struck by this appalling tragedy finds herself under immediate police suspicion. In a recent court case, which vindicated the mother of two babies who had died in this way, a doctor declared that the mother must be assumed guilty before being found innocent.

An American psychiatrist has even claimed that cot-death is the result of parents' failure to give their children enough love. Even if there were a shred of truth in that, how could a mother ever prove she had loved her child 'enough'?

The other professional arena in which children are continually assessed – that is, school – can also be a minefield for mothers. I have seen the most capable and cheerful of mothers quail at the prospect of meeting their children's educators at parent-teacher evenings. These mothers dread hearing about their children because they feel they are to blame when their child is less than entirely perfect. A parents' magazine calls this phenomenon 'Fright Night for Parents'.

Sadly, it is sometimes mothers who contribute to blaming other mothers. A friend told me rather ruefully that since her daughter had started going to school, she felt that her housekeeping, her child's packed lunches, even the child's dress and neatness were under scrutiny from other women. She felt as if she had to keep up to some ideal standard, or she would be putting her daughter at a disadvantage, marking her out as one less likely to succeed in life. That public judgement in itself would make her one less likely to succeed in life.

This gives people other opportunities to blame mothers – for being too competitive. The double bind is there again: if you don't keep your child in perfect condition, you are harming her chances in life. But if you're too keen to make her perfect, you're pushy, over-ambitious, competitive. When women are given credit for channelling their energies into more diverse kinds of work, when less cruel penalties are exacted from women for being less than perfect mothers, maybe women can relax a bit more. Until then, mothers are on a losing wicket.

The 'guilty womb'

Mothers' guilt for the shortcomings of their offspring is extended retrospectively not only into pregnancy, but also into their lives before conception. It is true that a woman has a better chance of having a healthy baby if she herself is healthy, but it is the way this message is conveyed to women that makes us feel blameworthy. (That the good health of the father is also important to the conception of a healthy child has hardly been investigated, let alone publicized.)

Today, more and more attention is being paid to 'preconceptual care' – the importance of good health and diet in a mother-to-be.

It is right that women should know that smoking and drinking alcohol can harm their babies. Yet the campaigns aimed at women in the past have shown the smoking or drinking mother as being selfish and irresponsible, greedily, sluttishly, puffing and slurping away – without a thought in her pretty head for the poor infant being poisoned in the womb.

The truth is that it has been to the great financial profit of the drinks and cigarette manufacturers to get women hooked on their products long before their babies were so much as a gleam in the eye. Successive governments have also made a vast amount of money from the taxes on alcohol and tobacco.

What hypocrisy then to turn around to the same women – who happen to be carrying babies – and blame them for doing what huge amounts of pressure (advertising and otherwise) have been pushing them into for years on end. If governments and their officials are serious about women's and babies' health, why aren't they prepared to sacrifice a bit of their government revenue by making cigarettes and drink harder to come by, and dealing with some of the stresses that lead mothers to drink and smoke in the first place?

Even when mothers-to-be may feel they aren't doing anything 'wrong', there is pressure to make them feel that – if they really cared about their offspring enough – they could do it better. In the USA, 'experts' claim that mothers can stimulate their babies' perceptions and intelligence even before birth by playing music, tapping out rhythms and reciting poetry through the uterus wall.

It used to be that parents wanting the best for their kids would hope to send them to university after they left home. Now they are under pressure to set them off on the right track under tutelage from the University of the Womb – before they've even left their mothers' bodies.

Paula Caplan cites an American psychiatrist who made a name for himself by claiming that a pregnant woman's thoughts and feelings can cause lasting psychological damage to the child she is carrying. Perhaps it is true that prolonged anxiety and tension in a pregnant woman can affect her child – but what about some concern for the effects these will already be having on the woman's health?

Such claims of pre-natal culpability have been made in spite of strong evidence and plain common sense. These show that it is the long-term experiences of the growing child and the range of relationships she has with people that will affect her emotional development, rather than any single one-off trauma in the past of her pregnant mother.

Similarly, the once-fashionable theory about 'bonding' stressed the vital importance of the moment of birth for the forming of a healthy, happy relationship between mother and child. While no doubt the idea served as a useful antidote to the increasing mechanization of the birth process, it was often taken out of context and has made many mothers feel inadequate.

Many women simply didn't experience it: the moment of bonding was as elusive and oppressive to some as the obligatory orgasm of the '70s. The rapidly increasing numbers of women who have been giving birth by Caesarian section, often under anaesthetic, weren't even conscious for the moment of so-called bonding, a 'failing' which has unjustly plagued many of them ever since. Others, at the exhausted end of hours of labour, just didn't feel the dawn of everlasting love as soon as

103

they set eyes upon their red and wrinkled infant.

The idea that these women aren't 'bonded' or don't love their children simply for the lack of this magic moment is pure fairytale. Besides, the British upper classes have for generations raised their children on the very principle of breaking the 'bond' with the mother and giving children as young as possible into the hands of nannies. What's sauce for the goose . . .

Court verdict

On a far more sinister level, women are being found guilty in the courts for what went on in their pregnant bodies. The law is treating a woman's womb as an entity separate from herself, as the property of posterity and of society. She is seen as the vessel for children, and her unborn children take priority over herself.

In ancient times, before the male's role in the process of conception was understood, pregnancy and birth appeared to be an entirely female mystery and women commanded awe and respect for their capacity to create new life. That power shifted when men came to understand their own function in fertility, and to lay claim to their own offspring. Hence women's enforced sexual fidelity in marriage, so that men could be sure of their parenthood.

Today, in the wake of astonishing advances in modern medicine, a woman's control and role in birth is often drastically reduced. Indeed, she doesn't even need to be alive to give birth. The doctors can do it all for her – as in the case of the brain-dead mother kept alive on the life-support machine until her baby could be delivered by Caesarian section.

Meanwhile, in California, a mother has been jailed for neglecting her unborn child. She had started haemorrhaging and then waited for twelve hours before going to hospital. The baby suffered from brain damage and died: the mother was found guilty of its death.

In Britain, the Lords have ruled upon the case of a woman whose baby was taken from her into care because it was born addicted to methadone, the heroin substitute. She wanted her child back: they have found her unfit to have it back. This has frightening implications for all mothers whose lifestyles might one day be judged 'harmful' by a court.

According to a report in the *Observer* in January 1987 a British mother, also a registered heroin addict, lost her fifteen-year-old daughter into council care. The girl told a teacher that her mother took heroin; social workers stepped in and the case went to court. This was in spite of the fact that the family doctor described the mother as 'a good parent'.

Two American women have been made to have Caesarian sections against their will, according to Katherine Whitehorn in the *Observer* (November 1986) 'for the sake of the child'. And in Chicago a judge gave legal custody of the foetus to a hospital lawyer when the mother refused to give her consent to surgery. Whitehorn quotes an American specialist in medical ethics who says he has never heard of a vaguer crime than neglect to the foetus:

It gives you a license to do whatever you want to a woman.

CHAPTER 5

Behind the myth of motherhood

Carrot and stick

With the carrot of idealized motherhood ahead of them, and the awful stick of retribution for those who 'fail' threatening from behind, women are ushered into childbearing. Which is not to deny that many women do genuinely have a remarkable capacity and desire to be caring, loving and giving, a capacity that they may develop and express in motherhood. Simply, instead of genuinely rewarding the work of mothers and respecting their true worth, this society massively exploits them.

The ideological soft focus on motherhood provides a smokescreen for the fact that the Government will not pay to keep our health service, childcare facilities and schools up to scratch. Instead, they are forcing many mothers to take up the slack and return to the role of prime carer within the family. Cuts in community services have forced many women to stay at home in order to look after dependent parents, sick relatives and children. Even after the European Court ruled that Britain must change her discriminatory laws and pay women for this work, the Government changed the rules again to avoid paying tens of thousands of carers.

So bad is the exploitation of mothers in this country that we have been dubbed the Cinderellas of Europe. Even at the most basic level of financial support and social security, maternity provision in Britain is abysmally poor compared with that in other European countries.

To make things worse, our long-term prospects of supporting ourselves and keeping good jobs have been seriously undermined in recent years as women's employment rights have been weakened, making it more difficult to get paid maternity leave and more difficult for a woman to get her job back after having a child.

The very structure of paid work with its inflexible, office-based hours and the total inadequacy of childcare provision in this country help to keep mothers economically dependent. Having taken the great leap into motherhood, too many women find they have lost their previously hard-won foothold in society.

Childcare – a crying shame

There is still a strong feeling in this country that it is a shame for children to 'have to' go into childcare. It's related to the diehard notion that it's a shame for a wife to have to go out to work. If wives have to work (this kind of thinking goes), it's because their husbands can't properly support them. By the same token, if children 'have to' go into childcare it's because their mothers don't really want them.

Less than a third of people in this country are happy with the idea of mothers of young children going out to work, as the National Marriage Guidance Council discovered in a (1984) survey. 'If you can't look after them yourself', women are often told, 'then you shouldn't be a mother.' It's an attitude which completely ignores the fact that mothers and children have probably never been so isolated as they are today, and disregards the harm such isolation can do.

Part of the problem is that many people imagine 'the family' consists of dad out at work earning the 'family wage', and mum happy and fulfilled at home with the kids. But in fact women are now over forty per cent of the paid workforce.

That's not because they want 'pin money', but because their families depend on a second income. Were it not for mothers' earnings, some three or four times as many families would be living in poverty say the Family Policy Studies Centre. Nearly a third of all mothers with children under five now have paid jobs – and many more would like to have jobs.

This is true even when the jobs available to women are lousy ones. Many mothers have to work part time because of their domestic commitments. They find themselves stuck in low-paid ghettos of boring work, without status, without long-term benefits or security. Women still make up three-quarters of the low paid in this country.

And a growing proportion of families have either mum or dad to depend on – but not both. One in ten British families has a single parent as the head of the household, responsible for supporting all its members. In a further half-a-million households women are the sole providers because of the unemployment of their partners.

Yet, women's employment and women's expectations have changed much faster than social prejudices about childcare and a mother's role. The days when mothers could rely on the extended family network, or – in the middle classes – on the widespread system of servants for help with childcare and a break from the isolation of home are gone for most of us.

It's an unusually lucky woman today who can rely on relatives living nearby to help her, and the cost of childcare keeps it as a largely middle-class privilege rather than a common right. Nor are modern homes always the best place for a mother and child to spend their days. In the city, home may be a cramped flat. The only place for children to play may be a traffic-congested street. The country is not always safe for children either, with the dangers of cars in narrow lanes and the perils of farm machinery.

On the other hand, childcare can be of enormous benefit to children and their parents. Children enjoy and learn from playing with other youngsters and adults. They go into school better prepared for the social, intellectual and emotional challenges they will face.

Good childcare gives mothers a chance to keep a paid job, hold on to their income, their independence, their confidence, their social contacts with colleagues and their self-esteem. Or it gives them some leisure time to get out of the house and break their isolation. Given the numbers who suffer from depression after children are born, that's no small bonus. Childcare may also provide an opportunity for women to take up further education or job training.

Four decades after Dr John Bowlby's work on the dangers of separating children from their mothers, women are still trying to lay the ghost of his all-pervasive ideas (which often means challenging our own mothers on how we were brought up). The old 'maternal-deprivation' bogey has persisted, despite lack of evidence that children must never be parted from their (female) parent.

I can't help you, dear . . .

Professor Barbara Tizard has reported on the recent research on this subject for the *Thomas Coram Foundation* in 1986. She found that separation from their mother does not in itself cause damage to children, and that a gentle period of settling in and introduction to the childcarer can smoothe the potentially difficult transition.

She also found that the mother-child relationship is not the only one which is important to development. Small children can become very attached to, and learn a lot from, a number of different people – like fathers, family friends, siblings and other relatives. What's important is not so much who that person is, but how familiar, responsive and affectionate they are to the child.

Similarly, day care in itself isn't harmful to children: what matters is the quality of that care. In 1983 the prestigious US National Academy of Science reported its findings that, 'there is no conclusive research to suggest that mothers' employment *per se* . . . has consistent direct effects either positive or negative on childrens' development and educational outcome.' The Academy found that it is other factors – like poverty, poor childcare facilities and strife between parents – which are more likely to upset and hurt a child.

Good childcare also makes good economic sense. The more women that are in paid work the more women contribute to the economy and the more jobs that could be found for childcare workers. American research has shown that nursery education can pay for itself by reducing the need for special help for some children when they get older. It also makes it more possible for children from less privileged homes to compete on an equal footing with the better-off.

For all of these reasons we are now seeing an enormous demand for childcare facilities. Ninety per cent of parents with three- or four-year-olds want nursery places for their children, and nearly a half of parents with a child under three also want some form of childcare provision.

Yet instead of getting more childcare places, we are getting less. In 1983 fewer than a quarter of three- and four-year-olds in England got any nursery education at all. Local authority provision for the three and a half million under-fives is less than one per cent. Provision varies drastically according to where you live: some Conservative authorities provide virtually no place at all. Like primary school hours, nursery hours are usually between 9.30 am and 3.30 pm, making it difficult for parents whose working hours extend into the evenings.

School holidays are another headache for mothers in paid jobs. Gingerbread, the one-parent family charity, rang up eleven big city councils to ask about school holiday care for children. Most of them didn't have any, and even those that did couldn't tell the Gingerbread researcher anything about it. Instead they set her off on a wild goose chase through every department from education to amenities and engineering. In the echo of such a response, Gingerbread called their subsequent report 'I can't really help you, dear.'

110

Baby, you can drive my car . . .

Yet in spite of having a 'working mum' for our Prime Minister, Tory thinking has remained implacably opposed to providing adequate childcare on the basis that this is a family (i.e. a mother's) responsibility. Just as the Government has accused the unemployed of being work-shy, so they imply that mothers want to shirk their duty. This is how the one-time Secretary of State for Social Services, Patrick Jenkin, put it (1979):

If [nurseries] are made available at public expense too readily they can all too easily be seen as the expression of a philosophy which preaches that parents can do as they like and it is the duty of the state to look after the children.

Mothers, it appears, must on no account 'do as they like', or the social fabric will fall apart. Perhaps it would, Mr Jenkin. Perhaps it should?'

His is the kind of thinking that led the Government to introduce a clause into the 1980 Education Act. This removed the obligation that councils once had to provide some form of nursery education. Since then, full-time nursery places have been shrinking, the ration of children to nursery staff is rising, waiting lists for day nurseries and playgroups are getting longer all the time and charges have gone up. Public funds, grants and subsidies for childcare are shrinking too – despite a £2 million 'special initiative' for the under-fives, which hardly compensates for the other cuts.

To add insult to injury, parents whose children enjoyed the rare benefits of a workplace nursery have found themselves saddled with huge bills. In 1984 the Government decided that parents must pay tax on any contribution they get from employers towards childcare costs. Some parents using a London workplace nursery found themselves with tax demands of over £3,000 for up to six years back tax.

The Government's rationale for doing this was that workplace nurseries are an élitist concern and should be taxed

111

accordingly. Yet there are no such taxes on workplace canteens or sports facilities. Indeed, there is more support available for an employee's car – four times the level of subsidies – as for a company employee's child.

All the opposition parties are pledged to remove this tax and even some Tory backbenchers have found it hard to stomach. As Tory MP Tony Baldry put it:

Much of the flexibility at present in the labour market is brought about by the participation of women . . . How then is it sensible to erect a barrier to such flexibility by a fiscal device involving, in budgetary terms, such a small return to the Treasury.

In July 1986 up to thirty-five Conservative backbenchers planned to revolt against the Government in order to reduce the workplace nurseries tax. But at the last minute the Speaker decided not to debate their amendment to the Finance Bill: it was said that he wanted to speed up Parliamentary business before the Royal Wedding!

By contrast, the Canadian and American governments offer tax incentives to parents to encourage them to invest in childcare. American day nurseries are run by big companies in franchised chains – like fast food restaurants. Parents who pay for child care get tax relief, just as people paying for mortgages do in the UK.

Not that America is the great land of opportunity for parents. Less than one in two hundred US firms help parents to balance the demands of paid work and children. However, the US Bureau of National Affairs says that bosses do realize that change is in the air.

Some American and a few British firms have started to experiment with 'parenting' seminars, flexitime, telecommuting schemes, job sharing and with contributions to childcare. And when firms do back such schemes, they have found (as any mother could have told them), that the productivity of their employees goes up. These fortunate parents can concentrate on getting on with the job instead of having to worry about the welfare of their children.

Within the next decade, eight out of ten American women (in the twenty-five to forty-four age range) are expected to be in paid work. There is legislation on the books in America which will give mothers or fathers eighteen weeks leave to care for newly born, newly adopted or seriously ill children. And San Francisco has become the first city in the USA to pass a law which obliges developers of major new commercial offices to provide rent-free space for childcare – or to pay for childcare elsewhere.

As for Europe, six of our EEC partners already have established parental leave policies. But last year (1986) Britain vetoed an EEC draft directive on parental leave and leave for family reasons: these would have given both parents the right to three months' leave before a child's second birthday. Nine out of ten European countries provide leave for fathers. Britain provides none.

All in all, this country remains one of the worst providers of childcare in Western Europe. In contrast to Britain, other EEC countries have acted on the understanding that good childcare benefits children, mothers and the whole economy. France, Denmark and the Netherlands have state nurseries for thirty per cent of their under two-year-olds; in Britain we have none. And ninety-five per cent of their under-fives are catered for.

The great majority of small children in France receive free education from the age of three – although it's not compulsory until they are aged six. The schools are open for the full span of normal working hours, from 8 am until 6.30 pm, with care provided at the end of the formal school day. There are pre-nursery school childcare schemes as well, with financial support for women who need to use them.

Belgian children and their mothers benefit from nursery education too, as well as from a crèche system which caters for children under three whose mothers are single or in paid jobs. In Sweden a scheme is underway to integrate child centres, by combining care and education under the same government ministry.

113

To compound their childcare difficulties, British mothers are often discriminated against when they are looking for paid work. More than ten years have passed since the Sex Discrimination Act (1975) made it illegal to ask a woman about her childcare arrangements before offering her a job. Yet the Equal Opportunities Commission (EOC) says that it gets around half-a-dozen enquiries a month on this subject. That is a fifth of all the enquiries made on the subject of recruitment, and is likely to be just the tip of the iceberg. The EOC say that women who are asked questions about childcare arrangements during a job interview should tell their interviewer that such questions could be illegal, and should also think about taking up the issue with the EOC.

Maternity benefits who?

For all but the most privileged women, having a baby means having a lot less money – about £135,000 less according to the Family Policy Studies Centre in a recent report ('Babies and Money'). This is the estimated cost to a 'typical' woman who leaves her £7,000 a year full-time job to have two children. It involves her loss of earnings for shorter hours, lower rates of pay and time away from a paid job.

The report says that the direct cost of having one baby is about £30,000 for the child's first sixteen years, but the cost to its mother in giving up paid work is much higher. The Equal Opportunities Commission estimates that having children can cost women up to half of their lifetime's earnings.

The implications of this loss to mothers reverberate from the office to the bedroom. Because of the way that the world of paid work is organized we are literally worth less than men. They know this; we know this; our children know this. Without drastic improvements to childcare and maternity provisions, we haven't a hope of reaching equality with men.

Yet even at the most basic level, provision for mothers in

114

Britain has been sliding downhill, from bad to worse to hardly any. Ten years ago it seemed that we had at least a basis of benefits and rights which gave us financial security around childbirth and the chance to carry on with paid work. But now maternity provision is in crisis and we are seeing the biggest ever attack on mothers' rights.

The one across-the-board payment women had been getting, the maternity grant, was a derisory £25. It was intended as a lump sum towards the initial cost of a new baby. But it was allowed to shrink to a fraction of its original value, and didn't go very far towards the £1,000 which Mothercare estimate is the cost of essentials for a baby's first year. And that's not counting clothes. Nor did it look very healthy besides the £500 plus maternity grants which mothers in countries like France and Luxemburg can expect.

Considering the cost of having a baby today, the grant came as a rather sick joke, but not nearly as sick as the message that accompanied it: 'If unfortunately your pregnancy ended more than 11 weeks before the week in which you were expecting your baby ... you should return the girocheque.' In the pain and grief of miscarriage or stillbirth a mother must remember to send back a sum which only paid for a few nappies anyway.

Now the Government is abolishing the maternity grant altogether. This comes as part of the package of new proposals (April 1987) which leave many women with no financial help at all to meet the costs of a new baby. The grant will be to some extent replaced by a means-tested benefit, but for the future, maternity benefits will be available to only a minority of mothers.

The Maternity Alliance estimates that half a million women are losing out on a lump sum towards the cost of a baby and those with no recent work record who are not on very low incomes will get no maternity benefits whatsoever. Mrs Thatcher has in the past been dubbed the 'milk snatcher': now her Government is again abolishing free milk as well as vitamins for pregnant women and children in poor families.

115

Employed women have had maternity rights in this country – the right to maternity leave and maternity pay, the right not to be sacked for being pregnant – for just over a decade. Other maternity benefits date back to 1911. We have seen one small gain: paid time off for ante-natal care.

But almost every year since 1979, the Government has managed to erode some of the job protection which mothers need and to take away some of the funds granted to them. When women were first given job protection in 1978, they had the right to have a baby and keep a job, as long as they had already worked in that job for six months.

By 1985 the qualifying period had been extended fourfold, so that unless a woman had been in a job for two years she lost her rights to keep her job and so to maternity pay and leave. The 1980 Employment Act put further hurdles in the way of women getting their jobs back, making equal opportunities at work a distant dream. Only about one in ten of mothers goes back to the job she had before having her baby.

So much for motherhood on its pedestal. The reality behind the propaganda is that mothers are being remorselessly and stealthily undermined. It is a tactic as old as chivalry itself to tell women they are wonderful while keeping them powerless. The position that mothers are forced into by employers and the state is the modern application of the old adage 'Keep 'em barefoot and pregnant'.

The sense of being undervalued which mothers feel as a result of the absence of practical and financial support is bad enough in itself. But it creates further stress and confusion in the minds of women who had been persuaded that motherhood was ideal.

It also cuts women off from each other. The childless friends of mothers perceive the ideal and may imagine they are enjoying great rewards. But women without children are cut off from the reality of the state-sponsored experience of motherhood. These factors all contribute to the divisions between mothers and non-mothers, and to the divisions within mothers themselves.

Depressed? It's only 'normal' . . .

A few weeks after my daughter was born I wrote in my diary:

She is sometimes sweet, funny, appealing, endearing. But I have not fallen in love with her. Love has not come all at once – as some mothers have told me it did for them. Mostly, I am just exhausted.

Women stop and talk to me on the street. All want to look at her, want to compare notes with their own finest hour. I have joined a club. She is my badge of belonging.

But I don't really want to talk to other women with babies – I can't bear their joys and ecstasy. It makes me feel a guilty failure. I want to say I'm fed up with her, you can have her. The best moments of my day involve escape. I feel so crafty if I can leave her down for a while or engineer a walk on my own across the common – to see the beautiful trees, young couples, slim girls with breasts not leaking milk.

It shocks me now to remember that I felt this way, about a child who was wanted and planned for over a period of years and who is now the much-loved centre of our life. I thought of myself not as depressed, but somehow lacking in 'maternal instinct'.

For the first few months of her life I did all the things I was supposed to do for her, I tried my best to love her, she was never out of my mind and I could hardly bear to be parted from her – but there was a lead weight in my heart. Not until she was about three or four months old did the joy of her existence outweigh it – and not until then did I stop feeling so weary.

I'm only prepared to reveal these feelings – not without qualms – because I now realize that many, if not most, mothers do go through tremendous emotional upheavals after their children are born. Since then friends have sent us announcements of births of their babies with notes like this one attached:

We're delighted with the baby. But it can't really go on like this for much longer, can it? How do people cope?

117

Many mothers do experience quite unexpectedly negative feelings about motherhood, as well as the joyful ones that they looked forward to. Estimates and definitions of depression vary considerably, but at least one school of thought believes that three-quarters of all women in Britain and in America suffer either depression or acute anxiety after childbirth.

For a few mothers (up to two in a thousand), the reaction is so severe that they endure psychotic breakdown, sometimes with hallucinations or silent withdrawal from the world. They are usually treated in hospital with drugs and may recover within a few months, although they risk going through the whole ordeal again should they have another baby.

Far more common – in perhaps half of all mothers – are the 'baby-blues' which many a weary new mother experiences about three days after the birth. She feels down and weepy, but gets over it in a day or two.

But between these two extremes are the legions of women who suffer a long drawn-out depression as their babies grow into toddlers and schoolchildren.

Sheila Kitzinger, writing in the *Independent* (4 November 1986), estimates that up to a half of all mothers could be affected like this:

Some are put on a steady diet of tranquillizers by GPs; others see psychiatrists and are prescribed anti-depressants. Others again somehow get by, drained of energy, feeling trapped in motherhood and often convinced that they are complete failures. No one realizes they are depressed because no one has seen them not depressed for months. They rarely find their way into the statistics of mental illness.

Such feelings can last for years. One study (reported in Georgina Boulton's book *On Being a Mother*) showed that a third of all mothers in a working-class area of London were 'clinically psychiatrically disturbed' – up to six years after their babies were born. Another study showed that a third of women with children up to three years old had been 'significantly depressed' over the previous year.

Clearly, motherhood is a very difficult experience for a lot of women. Yet for years our painful experiences have been lumped together and labelled 'post-natal depression', to be explained in terms of hormones. Endorphin, which is the morphine-like substance in the blood of pregnant women, does suddenly drop after birth. But there is no proven link between this hormonal change and the kind of depression which starts or goes on long after the birth.

It is convenient (for relatives, health professionals, friends, even sometimes for mothers themselves) to deal with women's unhappiness and anger by putting it down to female biology. Blaming 'pre-menstrual tension' or the 'curse', saying women are 'menopausal' or 'post-natally depressed': it's tempting to find a physiological 'cause' to explain away often complex problems.

It is not threatening to see women's difficulties as biologically determined, because it means that there's no need for change: the error lies in women's bodies, not in the world we live in. The 'problem' can be treated with drugs. Please adjust your set, there is no fault in reality . . .

However, all women, mothers or not, are far more liable than men to mental and emotional illnesses. This is not because we are the weaker sex, intrinsically prone to illness, but because we live in a world which doesn't pay enough attention to the needs of women. Increasingly, women are questioning the established hormonal theories about depression in mothers, and asking whether this kind of depression is not simply a 'healthy' reaction to the conditions of motherhood today.

As Kitzinger puts it:

Post-natal depression and despair is no accident, nor an act of God. It is the direct result of a society which puts motherhood on a pedestal while disparaging and degrading mothers in reality.

Women grow up believing that they want to be mothers and that motherhood will be their insignia of true femininity, adulthood and respectability. Yet when they achieve their goal, they soon find that society doesn't really value their job. Their status has not improved: it has got worse. The baby was to be their proof of 'success' – yet its crying confirms their failure to be a proper mother. Instead of pink and blue paradise, they've got dirty nappies and broken nights. Yes, there are times of joy, tenderness and great happiness. But they never expected to feel such resentment, anger, guilt and inadequacy.

They may have had a fantasy of Happy Families, with the proud father there to help and share with the new baby. But when men are emotionally immature they may not be able to cope with the enormous changes that have happened in their home lives. Some new fathers find it hard to come to terms with the fact that they no longer seem to be number one in their woman's affections.

Instead of being able to rely on her man, many a new mother finds she has another, bigger baby making further demands upon her. Not only does she face the conflict between her own needs and that of her baby, but her man may be insistently tugging her emotional skirts in another direction. Why else do so many new fathers appear to collapse with a mystery illness when their new offspring are brought home from hospital?

As their children grow up, mothers are daily confronted with the painful knowledge that they and their children don't matter to the powers that be. Why else do governments cut their benefits, cut the funding of their health service and schools? Why else do designers and planners organize and build the world in a way that constantly puts hurdles in their path, making it difficult or impossible to get through doorways, up and down steps, into toilets – or even to get out at all.

Our society values production, not reproduction. Georgina Boulton quotes research evidence to show that women's self-esteem drops when they leave paid employment to go into motherhood. After ten years of bringing up children – a job without pay, without social recognition or respect – employers will tell a mother she has no qualifications or work experience.

The language which we use for those whose work it is to care for children reflects how little this society respects them. Mothers who have paid jobs outside the home are called 'working mothers' – an expression which obliterates from consciousness the fact that all mothers work. Those who don't have paid jobs are usually called 'housewives', defined in relation to a man, wedlocked to a building. The term describes possibly the most important job in the world, done for love, not money. But it's not something that girls and boys 'want to be' when they grow up.

As one housewife (Bryony Lavery) wrote to the *Guardian*:

Housewife is the name for a many-skilled, many-faceted job that very few of us aspire to. Executive, on the other hand, is the name for a many-skilled, many-faceted, absorbing job that many of us aspire to . . . Can you imagine a world in which a man might say modestly . . . 'No, I don't work, I'm just an executive'?.

Until the work that mothers do is accorded its true value, until mothers and their children know they are valued, women will continue to suffer illness and unhappiness after their children are born. That is bad enough for mothers, but nobody knows how bad that can be for their children.

CHAPTER 6

The price our children pay

The position of women, especially mothers, and that of children is closely linked in our society. We are worth less than men in financial terms as well as being generally more vulnerable physically. This lack of power – in relation to men – leaves women and children open to a range of parallel abuses.

In many ways children, like women, can't call their bodies their own. After a long history of beating our children, many British people still believe we should use corporal punishment in our schools, while the physical assault of children continues in countless homes.

Women, meanwhile, are constantly on the defensive against the threat of physical and sexual assault from men. Once married, a wife's body is her husband's property to the extent that, should he rape her, the law cannot be used against him. Women also have to defend hard-won rights over their own bodies in terms of contraception, abortion and reproductive rights.

Children have no political power, and are dependent on adults to defend them. Women – only comparatively recently allowed to vote – have far less political clout and representation than men, and Westminster is still very much a male club.

Children are barred from many public places, and excluded from adult conversations. Women are absent and unwelcome in many public places and are expected to listen to men.

'Children should be seen and not heard' as the saying goes: it might just as well apply to women. Children are loveable as they appear in the fantasy world of much television and advertising – sweet, biddable and in bed by seven. But NOT loveable when they cry, protest or express their hugely energetic natures.

It's a well-documented characteristic of patriarchal thinking to see women as childlike (and that's not a compliment), while women are frequently referred to as girls late into adulthood. Just as the child is seen as an uncompleted adult, the woman is seen as an uncompleted man. Eve made from Adam's rib is the child of the man, as the child is born of woman.

Like children, women are supposed to need protection for our own good, protection from the outside world and from our own weaker moral and intellectual capacities. The world of a child is not 'truth' in the eyes of the law: when children have been sexually abused the tendency has been to put it down to their fantasies. Women who accuse men of sexual abuse also know what it is like to be disbelieved by the law.

In the words of a judge who is quoted by the Children's Legal Centre magazine *Childright* (April 1986):

It is well known that women in particular, and small boys, are liable to be untruthful and invent stories.

Such views of women and children have long been used to justify controlling and confining them.

The irony is that the only power this society gives freely to women is power over children. Thus the comparatively powerless find themselves in sometimes complete power over the completely powerless. It's a situation which can't be good for women or for their children.

We hate kids

In any hierarchy, those at the bottom tend to get a raw deal, and despite a lot of cant about how British people love kids, our children get a very raw deal. Journalist Jenny Glew, who wrote the award-winning article entitled 'We Hate Kids' for

WOMAN magazine (November 1982), found that the hostility of our society to children comes as a great shock to new mothers. The reality of the situation first struck her when she went out collecting for a children's charity some years ago:

'Is it for animals?', the lady in the first house asked. 'Children? Oh, sorry, no.' She wasn't the only one either – the others might not have actually turned me away but they certainly reduced the size of their contribution.

Many is the mother who seethes with outrage as she is turned away from a place which won't allow children – but will allow dogs. I've been asked to leave a pub at lunchtime because of the presence of my baby, although she was fast asleep in a Moses basket at the time, while dogs – no matter how seedy or smelly – were permitted to stretch themselves out wherever they liked.

Although for a nation of so-called animal lovers we are none too kind to animals either, it often seems as if the British are more interested in pets than in small people. The popular press revels in a shock horror tale of cruelty to a small furry creature – much more commonly reported than the fact that a third of this country's children are growing up in poverty.

This was just one of the disgraceful facts about how we don't care for our young that came out of the 1985 Maternity Alliance conference called 'Poverty – A Crisis for Babies.' It was sparked off by Health Minister Kenneth Clarke who had questioned the usually undisputed link between poverty and infant deaths. (On the day of the conference it was announced that the Government was planning to abolish the maternity grant and to means test the maternity benefit – as they have done from April of 1987).

The official poverty line is set by supplementary benefit and, according to this measure, over half a million children were living in poverty in 1981. And despite the fact that we are having less children, the numbers in poverty are growing more and more.

124

Yet the *British Medical Journal* (4 May 1985) reports that most social researchers suggest the real poverty line should be forty per cent higher – which raises the numbers of British children in poverty to a staggering three and a half million in 1981. The younger the family, the worse the poverty tends to be. These days both parents are usually in paid jobs until the first baby arrives. Then the mother loses her income, just at the time when the family's costs are pushed up enormously.

For children, poverty is a serious threat to their health and survival. Twice the number of babies die at the poorest end of the social scale as at the richest. The gap narrowed towards the end of the 1970s, but now it is widening again. Compared to the rest of Europe, our infant mortality rates are getting steadily worse.

According to the Black report (Penguin, 1982), poverty puts children at risk most severely when they are very young – between a month and a year old. For every death in social class one in this age group, there are four deaths in social class five. One of the main causes of these tragedies is accidents. While mothers are often blamed – and blame themselves – for whatever happens to their children, the figures show that when mothers aren't poor their children are less at risk from this kind of injury or death. As Richard Smith writes (*BMJ*, 4 May 1985):

Imagine a mother living in a bed and breakfast hotel with her children. Not only is accommodation poor so that there are broken bannisters and broken glass, but also the primitive cooking facilities may be a couple of floors away, meaning that a mother may have to leave her older child while she takes the baby to fill his bottle.

Perhaps while she is away, the toddler falls and burns himself. Similarly . . . cooker and fire guards are expensive and mothers will naturally not choose to leave their children without food in order to buy them.

This doctor confessed that he had not previously thought about how poverty could cause accidents to children. It may be hard for comparatively well-paid professionals to understand

125

the reality of life for mothers without money. Hence the 'own goals' scored by health professionals who may – despite the best of intentions – upset a mother with advice which she simply can't afford to follow.

Infant emergency

If we really cared for mothers and their babies, would there be such a shortage of urgent medical care for infants? A third of babies referred to intensive care may not receive it, the Maternity Alliance reported to the 1984 House of Commons Social Services Committee. We need nearly to double the number of intensive care baby cots now provided in the Health Service.

In Britain thousands of babies die needlessly each year in hospitals which are lacking in basic resuscitation equipment – or which don't have the staff to run special care baby units which are lying idle. Many of these babies are born early and small to mothers on low incomes and in bad health. If the chances of survival were the same for these babies as for those born to our most affluent class of mother, three thousand lives a year would be saved.

Yet doctors throughout the country have been forced to turn babies away through lack of staff and equipment. Babies that could be saved are dying, others are being damaged and handicapped through lack of resources. The staff shortage in the field is acute, with double the number of nurses needed (*Guardian* 7 July 1986) – not surprisingly when they can expect to be paid around £6,500 a year for extremely stressful and skilled work. In many hospitals some three-quarters of their equipment has been paid for by fund-raising charities.

Despite the hard work and devotion of thousands of individual doctors and nurses in the Health Service, many women get the message that maternity isn't worth much as soon as they find out they are pregnant and come for antenatal care. Of all places where mothers are likely to need facilities for

126

children the ante-natal clinic is surely one of the most obvious.

Yet according to a Maternity Alliance survey, half of mothers find no provision for children at antenatal clinics. Invariably, too, there is the frustration and discomfort of waiting to see the doctor in what is often a most uncongenial, intimidating environment. The survey showed that a third of British mothers find their clinics to be both uncomfortable and unpleasant.

How differently women would feel about themselves and their forthcoming children if – as in some European countries – they left their ante-natal clinic with a tidy sum to put towards the expense of childbearing. Not only does this demonstrate appreciation and concern for mothers and their children, but it's excellent motivation for attending clinics.

At least in Britain our governments are consistent: they don't provide enough before, during or after childbirth. Even the small sums available for children have been under attack. Pressure groups have had to campaign hard in the 1980s to save child benefit and to stop the Government from switching to a 'family credit' payment. The plan was to pay this through the wage packet – which would often mean to fathers instead of to mothers. But it would not go to fathers who were on strike – thus bringing children in as a weapon to impose industrial discipline on their parents. Fortunately, widespread opposition combined to defeat the scheme.

We have had some form of family allowances since the second world war. Campaigners like Eleanor Rathbone had long been arguing that such a benefit should be universal and by right:

Children should receive a little share of the national income given to them not in respect of their father's service in industry but in respect of their own value to the community as its future citizens and workers.

In 1946 the first family allowances were paid to all mothers for every child except the first. The principle had been established, but the story of the benefit since then has been a sad and shoddy one. For twenty post-war years the allowances were neglected until family poverty was 'rediscovered' and the Child Poverty Action Group (CPAG) set up to put an end to it.

Family Allowances were back on the agenda as CPAG set out to persuade the new 1964 Labour Government to take proper care of the nation's children. They thought it could be done within a year – but Harold Wilson was evasive and their optimism was dashed. By 1970 CPAG were attacking the Labour Government's lack of action and claiming that the 'poor had got poorer under Labour'.

Things got no better under the Heath administration, which saw no increases at all in family allowances, but instead a huge increase in means-testing and growing inequalities. The next Labour Government introduced the child benefit. But even then a Cabinet leak (passed on to *New Society* by CPAG) revealed that ministers were manoeuvering to postpone the benefit. The subsequent embarassment forced them to get on with it.

Mrs Thatcher's election in 1979 put benefits to children under unprecedented attack. According to Stewart Lansley of CPAG:

Since then the poor have been on the receiving end of some of the most inegalitarian social and economic policies since the war. In this climate – much tougher than in the early years – CPAG's role has inevitably been defensive, mobilizing opinion against cuts in benefits . . . The [current] Social Security Bill adds up to the most serious attack on the social security system since the war.

In their latest Divided Britain campaign, CPAG claim that, since Mrs Thatcher's rise to power, the rich are £2 billion better off as a result of tax cuts, whereas the poor are £2 billion worse off as a result of cuts in benefits. Those facts have a grim significance for the third – or more – of the nation's children who now live in increasing poverty.

When does a child become a human?

At the root of all this is a deep malaise which doesn't even have a name in our language – unless it be 'childism'. For the unpalatable truth is that many people don't particularly consider or care about children because they don't really think of them as people. Like racism, sexism or ageism, this is a way of distancing others who are not like 'us', a way of not having to feel or bother about them.

People talk about children, especially small children and babies, in a way that they (if 'liberal') wouldn't dare to talk about ethnic minorities or disabled people. The same individual who wouldn't dream of saying 'I don't like Blacks/women/old people/the disabled' will quite confidently declare 'I just don't like children'.

This statement is often accepted without surprise or disapproval. It even wins a kind of deference to the preferences of the anti-child individual. 'Oh sorry', thinks the beleaguered mother, 'I'd better make sure the kids don't annoy you,' – even if she's also feeling 'you nasty so and so . . .'

Child psychologist Valerie Yule has been asked in all seriousness by young parents, 'When does a child become human?'. The answer in the minds of many people seems to be – not until he or she is old enough not to be a child any more.

In August 1986 *Woman* magazine interviewed a Cabinet Minister about a day he had spent with some young people on a drug rehabilitation scheme:

They're yobs if you like, but when you treat them as human beings they become articulate and bright as buttons.

The person referring to these not-quite-humans is Kenneth Baker, Minister for Education of all our not-quite-humans.

Whereas other oppressed groups can organize and speak out in their own defence, children are reliant on adults to defend them. This is why the Children's Legal Centre is

129

arguing that Children's rights must be seen as an important issue:

Children are, as yet, rarely recognized as having a right to have their views considered, or their interests independently represented at all levels of decision making – in Parliament when changes in legislation are proposed, in courts when decisions are made about their future, and in other places, where issues affecting young people's lives are settled.

The Children's Legal Centre has recently complained to Normal Fowler, Secretary of State for Social Services, about the continued use of solitary confinement as a way of punishing and controlling children in care. In one case, a young woman in care was stripped by a male member of staff, in order to force her to wear night clothes so that she would be unable to run away. He took off her jumper and pants. She objected and clawed him in the face. She was prosecuted for assault and sentenced to six months youth custody. Because she was in care and fifteen years old she had no defence against having her clothes removed by this man.

Our society's refusal to treat children as fully human is quite blatant in attitudes towards corporal punishment of children. Take the case of the Nottingham schoolboy Stephen McKevitt. In 1984, Stephen's woodwork teacher caused injuries to his neck and windpipe 'compatible with being forcibly grabbed around the neck' – as his family doctor put it.

The teacher received a caution from the police, but was not prosecuted. Yet when the boy's father hit the teacher, the father was prosecuted for assault and fined. Do we really believe that it's not acceptable to hit an adult, but OK to hit a child? Eighteen months later the Criminal Injuries Board awarded damages to Stephen McKevitt of £200: this is less than the amount of his father's fine.

The degree of power that adults have over children in schools is being increased by the new Education Bill. Whereas the Bill is designed to give parents more power in school government, it entirely excludes children from having any effective say in how their schools are run. In the past, some local education authorities did include young people under eighteen as members of their school governing bodies. But once the Bill is implemented even these few young people will lose their places. The Junior Education Minister Mr Bob Dunn has told Parliament that 'a school governorship is an office of public and pecuniary trust and thus may not be properly held by a minor.'

It has been proposed – but rejected by Mrs Thatcher – that the way to improve the lot of our children is to create a Minister for Children. She replied (January 1986) that this wasn't necessary, as 'all matters concerned with the welfare and protection of children' are under the Minister for Social Services. We have all seen what has been happening to our social services. Don't our children deserve better than that?

Behaving like a child?

It's not just in our institutions that we treat children without respect, but on the public street. We have all seen parents losing their tempers with children in public, and those of us who are mothers may have excused them mentally in memory of how tough it can sometimes be.

A study carried out by Valerie Yule paints a grimly consistent picture of our regular rudeness to children in this country. She watched individual adults out on the street with one child, and compared their social behaviour with that of pairs of adults in the streets. While she found that individual adults are almost always courteous towards each other on the streets – communicating with smiles, talking with each other, looking at each other – she found that adults don't talk to their children, don't smile at them or look at them. Adults will also publicly shout, cuff or yank at the arms of their offspring with offensive ill temper and irritation.

She saw children scolded and smacked, pulled out of push-chairs without warning, ignored while they cried or pacified with sweets. Within a two-minute period of being observed, only a quarter of adults had any communication with their children at all. For two-fifths of her sample 'pairs', what took place between them was negative:

For the rest, the adults took no notice of the children they were with, even in some pairs that I watched for up to ten minutes. The most typical adult-child couple consisted of a young woman staring ahead with a sombre face, as if tuned in to some dumb misery of her own (which must surely affect the child), while the child walked, sat, lay or was carried with a blank expression on its face. (*New Society*, 27 September 1985)

This is where – for children – the desperate undervaluing of motherhood comes home to roost. Little wonder if many of today's mothers are sombre. The misery they are tuned into comes surely from the conditions of manmade motherhood. It comes from the knowledge that faces them as they cajole, propel or 'yank' their children about the street, on and off the buses, through the heavy doors and along the narrow shop corridors that there is virtually nowhere they can go where they are welcome except for the isolation of 'home'. It comes from mothers feeling that they are not valued; and as the mothers are made miserable, so are the children.

Britain's Bijou Belsens

If British people treat their children badly in public, then the damage, injury and even death which some parents (mostly male) inflict on them in private defies description. In 1986 Childline, the free telephone helpline service for children in trouble or danger, was launched by the BBC after Esther Rantzen's *That's Life* revealed unexpected levels of unreported child abuse.

In the first two days of Childline over 12,000 children called. Since then some 10,000 children a day have been trying to get through. Only about 500 a day are successful; the others hear a recorded message which encourages them to keep trying.

Even the Childline team have been shocked by the extent of children's need. Paul Griffiths, Childline's Director has said they expected to be answering 500 to 800 calls a month – not that number each day.

'Let's face it', said Esther Rantzen who helped launch the project, 'there are Bijou Belsens in our country where there is a level of pain inflicted systematically on children.' (*News of the World* 30 November 1986)

The recent unprecedented publicity about child abuse – as well as affecting the figures of reported cases – has brought a shocked awareness to people in this country that abuse is not a rare and freakish thing perpetrated by unnatural monsters. It is a fairly common part of British family life. At least three children a week are killed by their parents, say the NSPCC, and many of these crimes are never discovered. Since 1979, reported physical abuse of children has nearly doubled. The NSPCC estimate that over 7,000 children a year in England and Wales suffer from physical abuse, although the proportion who are seriously injured or killed has declined. Small children are the most vulnerable, especially to abuse that causes head injuries like fractured skulls and brain damage. Ninety-four per cent of children with this kind of injury are under five.

But most cases of child abuse are not spectacular: they are not even visible. Neglect of children can take many forms and the more subtle cruelty of emotional maltreatment, neglect and sexual abuse are rapidly on the increase.

One child in ten in this country may be the victim of sexual abuse, according to a MORI survey (VOLCUF's publication *Co-ordinate* Spring 1986), and the proportion of children to suffer from some form of abuse could be as high as one in five. That suggests a serious problem in practically every other family in the country.

Britain thinks of itself as a 'civilized' nation, yet our child abuse record together with that of some other Western industrial nations is considered scandalous by the rest of the world. It is notoriously difficult to make comparisons with other countries as there are many different standards of what constitutes abuse and many different ways of recording it. Yet while countries as different as China and Scandinavia are reputed to have little or no abuse, Britain ranks as one of the world's worst abusers of children.

This is true even though our standards of what constitutes abuse are not of the highest. We record cases of physical injury and of emotional and sexual abuse committed by an individual against a child. But we don't examine what organizations (police, medical institutions, group homes) or social institutions may do to damage – or to fail to protect – children.

In contrast some third world countries use a much broader definition, including the effect of society and the environment on a child's health and development. Uniquely, third world researchers consider the plight of the hungry and include 'nutritionally battered children' in their statistics. They also count as child abuse the impaired development or death of children from adverse environmental factors which are preventable in the light of scientific know-how and adequate health care.

Unfortunately there are virtually no cross-cultural studies on child abuse, which makes detailed comparisons between cultures difficult. But the overall picture is clear: child abuse and violence towards children is a problem of the developed, industrial world. It is comparatively rare in the developing nations, although where countries are being 'developed', child abuse becomes a problem.

Wherever there is rapid social change which affects the structure of the family, tribe or community (as has happened in African countries recently), children soon feel the brunt of their parents' difficulties. It seems we export our social problems along with our Western ways of doing things.

134

Responsibility without power

So what have these child-friendly cultures got that we haven't? The answer could be that they have more tolerance and respect for the humanity of their children. According to the journal *Child Abuse and Neglect* (vol. 7, 1983), which reviewed the international literature on the subject, 'abuse is less likely to take place in societies which have strong positive cultural values attached to children.'

But you don't have to go to the third world to find a society that cares for children – as the Scandinavian example proves. Here the definitions of abuse vary again, but some definitions include even spanking and humiliation of children as abuse. So why does child abuse seem to be so rare in Scandinavia? According to the same journal, it is because of 'values placed on children' and 'the cultural appropriateness of using violence as a means of social control'.

In Sweden it seems, it's just not on to hit children as a way of imposing one's will upon them. If that's still a silly notion to British people, then perhaps its time we changed our notions. After all, not so long ago men assumed they had a right to keep their wives under control in the same way.

It's not just our values that determine how we treat children. The levels of stress that people live under make an enormous difference too. There can't be a mother in existence who hasn't felt she might lash out at a child when times are tough. No doubt there are thousands of parents in this country who are racked with guilt and self-hatred for what they have done to their children at the instant when love was eclipsed by the strains of life.

Bad social conditions harm parents who then harm children. Unemployment and debt are two of the chief trigger factors for child abuse, say the NSPCC, together with marital discord. And unemployment is looming larger as a cause all the time; in 1984, over two-thirds of fathers of abused children were unemployed.

135

When it is mothers who are doing the abusing, the fact that a mother doesn't have a job outside the home makes her far more likely to harm her children. NSPCC figures for the first half of the 1980s show that less than fifteen per cent of such mothers were employed outside of the home, while nationally, half of all mothers of dependent children go out to work.

Contrast the generally good social conditions in the Scandinavian countries: women have access to freely available contraception and abortion – which means women don't have to have babies when they don't want them. Premature babies are cared for in special wards and only released once their parents have been properly instructed in how to care for them. Thousands of newborns in the UK, however, are dying from lack of resources in the Health Service.

The rarity of child abuse in Scandinavia is also linked to the fact that many mothers work and leave their babies in day care institutions. British mothers have been hounded by the idea that going out to a paid job is damaging to children – yet the evidence clearly suggests that the reverse is true.

In the light of what women say about the shock of becoming a mother – our ignorance of the realities of motherhood and the isolation of being lost in unknown waters – it is significant that another prime cause of child abuse cited by the NSPCC is 'unrealistic expectations of the child'.

In the past five years the NSPCC has changed its method of recording the stress factors behind child abuse in order to include the state of the relationship between parents and children. 'Inability to respond to the maturational needs of the child' is now frequently quoted as a stress factor, together with 'inability to deal with "normal" child behaviour'.

In other words, many British parents don't know what parenthood is going to be like, they don't know how to deal with the problems of children growing up – and they don't know what 'normal' childhood is all about. And when they've got no job, no money and they're rowing with their partner, they take it out on the smallest, most vulnerable person around.

136

The 'unrealistic expectations' fostered by the idealized version of motherhood set up difficulties and divides which damage not only mothers but their children. And the social conditions of man-made motherhood – which confer responsibility without power – are putting such stress on parents that child abuse is becoming a part of our way of life. The only encouraging thing about this situation is that these are things that we can – and must – change.

CHAPTER 7

That disabled feeling

Stories for girls

Doesn't every happy pregnant woman have a glowing fantasy of what it will be like when she takes her baby out for the world to see?

Resplendent in the pram the Perfect Baby lies, gurgling and cooing at the affectionate strangers who lean smiling to welcome its existence. And as she pushes her newborn around the park in the sunshine, the mother's heart is bursting with pride in the sure knowledge that all about her must be filled with wonder – as she is – that such a precious new life has been brought into the world . . .

Unfortunately, this glowing fantasy usually remains a fantasy, for while the mother may well be madly in love with her infant, she rapidly finds out that the rest of the world isn't. Nor does it show any signs of being particularly proud of her either.

Even when her fantasies have been of the humbler kind, involving simple kindness from others, she is likely to be disappointed. For rather than emerging from her confinement as a person whose new responsibilities demand consideration, the new mum is more likely to feel that she has suffered a serious handicap. Indeed mothers talk about 'that disabled feeling' which comes over them when first they venture into the outside world with their children.

Forget the fantasy. 'A Mother's Real Life Adventure Into the Outside World' is more likely to read like this:

Up at dawn to prepare equipment (nappy bag, shopping bags, snacks and drinks for children, reams of tissues) and muster expedition (several hours necessary to wash and feed children, to dress, possibly change again, find matching shoes, gloves etc). The mother is already worn out and she's only about to leave the house.

Sets out to take elder child to school, accompanied by baby in her buggy. All three must jink and dodge through the urban dogdirt (people would look on in horror should the child – taken short – need to squat at the edge of the road). Through the lead-laden exhaust fumes discharging themselves at exactly the level of the babies' face, the mother takes her eldest to school and heads for the shops.

Via the Post Office to get her child benefit – but she can't get up the steps with her buggy. Unencumbered, hurrying people bound up and down the steps, but no one stops to help her lift her load. She finds a side entrance up a ramp, but the doors are so heavy that she risks the baby being cut in half unless someone comes along to hold them open.

Baby gets fractious in the queue and mother escapes for the shops with relief. In the department store the buggy hardly fits between the rails of clothes and she can't sidestep the other shoppers in the way. Resists temptation to use buggy as battering ram and retreats to supermarket.

Pushing a buggy and supermarket trolley (as no cradle available for baby) requires four arms, but she makes it to checkout eventually where other mothers are struggling to restrain their angry, frustrated and often screaming toddlers from eating the sweets placed carefully at their eyelevel. She sees a wide 'Disabled' till. No Mothers' till, however.

A sit down and a drink is now needed to revive body and spirit, but the coffee shop is upstairs and the pub won't let the baby in. Strategy: get bus home rapidly before baby gets too hungry/wet/bored.

To late. Baby is wet, wants a feed, cries. People at the bus stop stare. If she's very lucky there's a toilet or shop nearby with a mother and baby room where she can change or feed. But if not she's got two options: lay the baby down in public on the ground to change it, or leave the nappy till she gets home.

As for the feed, if it's a bottle or snack, that's feasible (if she remembered to bring it), but breastfeeding? Virtually impossible until she gets home.

As the bus pulls up she has only seconds to extricate the baby and fold the buggy, while clutching baby and shopping. The bus then lurches off again as she totters on the step with no hands free to break a fall. Drops shopping while trying to get change out of purse and find seat. No special seats allocated for mothers.

Baby – jolted and jostled as bus lurches on – has possetted on shoulder and is still crying. Other passengers frown or look away – except for another mother who smiles in sympathy. Not far to home, not far now to the safety of her own four walls, where there may be no one else to talk to but at least there's no one else to make her feel unwelcome.

The End.

It certainly feels like the end, but in fact is only the beginning. For if mothers are to lead even the semblance of a normal life there are a host of other places in the outside world that they need to go to and where they will feel just as uncomfortable in the company of their children.

We're getting there

Getting there is usually at least half the battle. Not many children will sit still or sleep for more than a few hours at a stretch in a car, and it can be very frustrating and upsetting for a mother to be stuck in traffic or on the motorway. From the driving seat she can't attend to the needs of her child crying in its seat at the back of the car.

She is worried and distressed by the child's distress, and the child probably thinks it is being punished for some obscure, unjust reason – which could be what much of its childhood feels like in this country.

Alternatively, mothers can travel by bus or coach. But narrow steps, high doors and the palaver of taking babies out of prams and buggies – together with the hostile attitudes of other passengers and staff – are enough to put one in five mothers off using buses altogether, according to a *Woman* survey. A further twenty-five per cent of mothers avoid using buses unless it's absolutely necessary.

Well, there's always the train – for the woman that can afford it. And/or for the woman who can endure the classic mini-drama that invariably ensues as she enters the carriage with her child. She knows that every individual in that carriage who is sitting next to a spare seat is praying and pleading with Fate not to lead the mother to that seat.

Too bad. Someone will have to put up with it. If she's lucky she'll find another mother whose children will entertain hers and who will understand about nappies and feeding and child exuberance. If not, she faces several hours of guilty misery under the silent onslaught of the public's disapproval.

After all, the advertisements tell us, people take the train to take the strain – to lay out their briefcases on the table, to unfold the Daily Outside World and stretch out their legs. Except mothers that is.

The most reasonable thing for the mother to do is to head straight for the virtually empty first class, plonk her retinue down on the extra spacious seating and begin spooning out yoghurt.

Unfortunately, British Rail are likely to take exception. So are the businessmen who are paid-up first-class people. Perhaps BR could improve the situation by creating a third class of ticket for mothers and children? It might encourage the third of mothers who say they never travel by train.

Alternatively, they could improve their services on the European model. BR have used the excuse that, unlike many in Europe, our stations were not destroyed in the war and so are more old-fashioned. But not all our stations are pre-war, and even if they were it shouldn't cost a fortune to adapt a few station loos or waiting rooms to include mothers and baby rooms.

Until then British mothers have to change their babies' nappies either on the train floor – which is not only unhygienic but unsafe – or on the passenger tables. That's the kind of circumstance which makes one in three mothers decide they won't travel by train (*Woman*) – and which also give the public a reason to beef about mothers.

When in November 1982 *Woman* magazine compared our train service to that on European railways, they found that many continental trains are likely to offer special family compartments, safety straps for carry cots, space for prams on the train and special baby changing facilities in the toilets such as pull-down changing flaps.

But even when transport facilities are modernized, the planners tend to forget the needs of mothers and children. This is despite the fact that women, who are in the minority of car drivers, are most likely to have to use public transport.

On the London tubes, for instance, the huge stretches of escalator at some stations make them a no-go area for women with prams and buggies; and the ticket-collecting machines seem especially designed to snap their barriers shut behind one's back – and just at head level of the toddler in tow. Of course, mothers can make the detour to go through the other barrier with a ticket collector – confirming that whoever planned the station didn't consider mothers to be part of the 'normal' passenger traffic.

You've got there

And what happens once a mother has thankfully arrived at her destination? Can she relax and get on with what she wants to do? Not likely.

Most venues of the adult world are alien and hostile to her if she is in the company of children. Of course, there are places – like offices – where the majority of people would agree children simply shouldn't be. That consensus is itself rather a sad reflection on the extent to which we have divided the life of home from that of 'work', but even if we accept it there are still occasions on which mothers and children do have to go into offices.

I have worked in one office with a large female staff, many of whom had problems with finding care for their children at the end of the school day, at half-terms or holidays. On a few occasions when childcare arrangements broke down, children were delivered into their mothers' hands at work before the end of the office day. Very soon management distributed a memo to staff, instructing that on no account should children be seen in the office.

There's more at root here than the office workers' natural irritation at being distracted by the noise a child might make. There are firms that make money from selling things to people in offices – like the London company that employs young women to sell shirts to businessmen at work. This business literally trades off some businessmen's love of being distracted from their work – if distracted by an attractive woman.

No, the whole world of the office is deep down hostile to the whole world of mothers and children. The dearth of workplace nurseries in this country – there are only about seventy all told – reflects the lack of interest at work about who cares for the children. Not that such nurseries don't have their drawbacks, but the absolute division between home and the office has made motherhood invisible at work. According to Marion Kozak of the National Childcare Campaign there is a widespread blindness at the workplace to the whole issue of childcare, even amongst women workers:

Those women who are at work don't see a problem. Or else they tend to have the attitude that 'If I can do it, then they can do it.' Even in nurseries I have heard workers complain about working at times like Christmas Eve: they say 'these mothers, you would think they would want to be at home with their children'.

Ms Kozak believes that many people still assume all such childcare difficulties will be absorbed by 'the family'. But 'the family' is a largely illusory concept which bears little relation to the reality of how most of today's real families operate.

The notion that childcare should be a 'family' responsibility and quite separate from the office is still widespread. When some years ago the trade unionists at a large publishing company tried to gauge the support of the largely female staff

143

for a company crèche, the response was mostly negative. Some people commented that childcare was a private matter and nothing to do with the company.

Relax, don't do it . . .

And what of the other venues where adults go to relax and recuperate from the world of work? Today's mother knows that in order to remain in touch, in shape and in good spirits she must keep up her recreational activities and social contacts. Yet there aren't very many public places she can go to unless she finds someone else to look after the children. But if she's left the children in someone else's care all week while she goes out to earn a living, she may not want to leave them behind again.

Few sport or leisure centres in this country have a crèche. Yet even as mothers ease themselves out of their hospital maternity beds they are faced with posters urging them to Keep Fit! Get Back in Shape! Look after the Figure! But where? How? Not to mention 'Why?'. When my baby was small I telephoned every swimming pool and leisure centre within reach of home – then south London. I couldn't find one with any provision for minding children. I ended up nervously leaving my sleeping babe in the office of the friendly lifeguard at the local pool, raising my head after every length to listen for imagined cries. Very relaxing. In 1986 the London Women's Handbook was published by the GLC's late Women's Committee. It listed forty sports and leisure centres; one in six provided some sort of crèche at specific times of the week.

Then there were the abortive tennis games at local parks with friends. We tried putting the poor child in her pram at the edge of the court until we realized a stray ball could practically decapitate her. Meanwhile the Dobermans and Alsations roaming the rest of the park together with my city paranoia about some weirdo kidnapping her made it impossible to put the pram outside the court. Besides, such half-baked strategies are only possible for as long as a child is very small and also asleep.

So if a mother gives up trying to keep fit and heads for the pub, it is only to find that she is relegated to the garden with other parents in a little social-leper colony. That is, only for as many days as the English summer light and weather will allow. Nor is she welcome with her child in wine bars or restaurants, unless the managers happen to be Greek, Indian, Chinese, Thai, Italian – in short, anything but English. And unless a fair proportion of the other customers are also from other more child-friendly climes.

Why not, cry the traditionalists? A pub or restaurant is no place for a child anyway. That appears to be true, but only because British people have decided that it should be so. It's certainly not so on the Continent, where UK travellers are astounded to see whole families sitting down to eat and drink together. Other cultures actually welcome children as people in their own right, and if they stay up long past the British bedtime then its because the adults are enjoying their company.

As for the theatre, the ballet, the opera or the cinema, forget it. These places really are not for women with small children. The loss of this kind of culture and entertainment is something that most mothers accept as one of the temporary sacrifices it is worth making in order to have children. Until someone somewhere starts sounding off about how boring mothers are with nothing to talk about except their children and what they've seen on television . . .

Lets go to the shop

Most mothers, in the depths of their humility, don't really expect to be welcomed into the places where people without children go. It's probably just as well. Yet surely they can expect to feel safe, comfortable and easy in the places where they are supposed to go – like the shops.

Not so. Even though women are the chief consumers in our

145

society, our shops are often designed without consideration for the fact that many of those women will be in the company of young children. That means that women need access to lavatories, to changing and feeding facilities. They need to be able to get through doors that won't swing shut on a pram or toddler, and to get into a shop without having to negotiate steps or flights of stairs. In big shopping centres they need pram parks, and often a seat for a child in a shopping trolley.

Some progress has been made in recent years, but often it seems to be the campaigns for the disabled that have scored successes – for example, wide tills, ramps and improved access – which happen to benefit mothers too.

Much of today's buying takes place as families set out once a week to do a big shop at the local supermarket. The supermarket chains are keen enough to take mothers' money, but they still prove rather reluctant to invest in facilities which will make shopping less of an ordeal for mothers.

Mother magazine (September 1986) ran their own consumer survey of supermarkets by sending out a mother plus toddler plus baby to a selection of the largest and newest stores around. 'Even so,' they concluded, 'the results add up to a pretty poor deal for mums. And we know only too well that in smaller and older stores the services and facilities may be much worse.'

Less than half of these new superstores had trolleys with any kind of baby cradle. The majority were also lacking in toilets which mothers could use for the inevitable toddler emergency. Only two out of seven supermarkets provided toilets. Mothers also found razor blades within children's reach at checkout counters, sweets invariably on tempting display at the checkouts, minimal help only reluctantly given with packing and a widespread lack of baby changing facilities.

The more positive side of the *Mother* survey's findings concerned the quality and choice of food available – an aspect which benefits the sales figures of the shop as much as the people who go there to spend. They also approved of the big new automatic doors in many supermarkets which do make life easier for mothers, and commented that attitudes seem to be improving as most of the shops were helpful in finding items for mothers.

We're still lagging a long way behind many other countries which offer services like properly supervised crèches and nurseries in shopping centres, plus play areas for older children. Such initiatives are very rare in this country, even in purpose-built consumer palaces like Milton Keynes. Despite its one mile of brand new shops, it started life without any supervised play area.

Contrast the facilities available to Australian mothers in places such as Sydney. For years now mother and baby rooms have been widely available with changing facilities, kettles, bottle warmers, high chairs and breastfeeding cubicles. Every suburb has a Women's Amenity Centre which offers the same kinds of facilities.

Yet there are some healthy – if slow – changes underway in this country. Mothercare have recently opened their first crèche in their Worcester store. It caters for two- to six-year-olds and is supervised by qualified nannies. Children can stay there for two hours at a stretch for a cost of £1.25 an hour. It has different play areas, a Wendy House and a 'Quiet Corner' for children who want to rest and look at books.

To date, 143 Mothercare shops also have mothers rooms where women can change and feed their children in safety and comfort. What a relief it is to retreat from the hurly-burly of shopping into this oasis where it is possible to give an uncomfortable child the care and attention it needs. The smaller shops don't always have such a room, but mothers are usually welcome to go to the staff room. What is still widely missing are loos, which all mothers with toddlers need access to if they are out for more than an hour or so.

Making strides

A campaign has recently been organized by a joint working

party with members from the Royal College of Midwives, the National Childbirth Trust, the La Lèche League and the Health Visitors' Association together with the Association of Breastfeeding Mothers, with Mothercare as the sponsors, to encourage premises to display a special national Babycare symbol – of a mother cradling a child – to show that they have facilities for mothers and children.

The Babycare symbol can be displayed where a shop or restaurant provides facilities for mothers which are within minimum standards of cleanliness, warmth and privacy. Mothers must also have somewhere to sit plus washing facilities with paper towels and waste bins. Anyone can contact one of the organizations involved in the campaign to ask them to check over a potential 'Babycare' premises. Once the symbol is awarded, the facilities will be monitored to check that standards have been maintained.

Many of the big stores are beginning to provide better facilities. In Manchester, for instance, an enthusiastic member of the NCT has managed to persuade all the big stores in the city to provide mother and baby rooms. And Peau Douce – the disposable nappy manufacturer – has sponsored a guide to hotels and restaurants in the UK which welcome children. Recently, Boots the Chemists have begun to open mother and baby rooms in their larger shops in over fourteen British towns. Restaurant chains like Little Chef and Happy Eater are also keen to welcome young families. Little Chef restaurants now offer free food for babies, and all of their 248 restaurants which are dotted along the country's motorways sell baby changing packs for 99 pence. Some of them are also installing better changing facilities as part of a pilot scheme. No doubt the huge success of the Macdonald's chain of restaurants has made their British rivals realize that it really can be worth making children welcome.

In many towns it is mothers who are taking the initiative, organizing self-help groups, lobbying local shops and businesses to take more care of mothers' needs – and publishing a flood of local guides for parents. In Bristol for instance, a group of mothers have produced the *Titch-hikers Guide to Bristol*, a handbook for parents with babies and young children packed with the kind of information which could only be gleaned by long experience of taking children out and about in that particular city. It tells you everything from how to change your doctor, to where you can breastfeed your baby in the city or find a pub that welcomes parents and children. It is a guide to finding playgroups, meeting like-minded parents and finding out about child development. The handbook even has the kind of rare, esoteric advice that at times is worth its weight in gold – like where to go to show your child a real pig, where to buy an inflatable potty or where to get your child's teddy mended.

The enormous success of the guide testifies to a great need and shows how mothers – from the beleaguered isolation of the family home – can benefit from mutual help and shared information. Liz Sherwood who helped to put the guide together (her own twenty-two-month-old daughter she claims constitutes a 'British Standard Test' for any amenities in the city), says that it has sold 4,000 copies in a year.

The Bristol women are not alone in their success; the Voluntary Liaison Council for the Under Fives (VOLCUF), say that over forty of these guides are now being published in different towns and that they are now compiling a guide to the guides, called *How To Do It*. Long may they proliferate!

Breast is for the birds

If there is one straightforward way to keep mothers in purdah, it is to ban them from breastfeeding in public. Over the past decade the numbers of mothers breastfeeding their children has gone up from half to some three-quarters – for very good reasons of their babies' health and good nutrition. That means that for at least the first few months of their children's lives, new mothers need to be able to breastfeed wherever they are, whenever their babies want to be fed.

But while breasts may be daily displayed on Page Three of the nation's newspapers, or 'streaked' across a cricket pitch in support of sportsmen, they may not be publicly seen to perform the function of suckling a child.

Many women find themselves 'taken short' in public and have no option but to take refuge in a toilet to feed. This doesn't do much for a mother's self-esteem, let alone provide the relaxed, comfortable and hygienic environment she needs. And it doesn't say much for our society's attitude towards children to condemn them to lunch on a loo seat.

A mother from Bristol wrote to *Woman* magazine (7 May 1983) about her experiences of going out with a new baby:

It was our first trip out with our baby girl. In a restaurant I took Pamela to the ladies' room. The toilets were dirty, blocked up and stank. There were no chairs, shelves or even soap. But Pamela couldn't wait so I ended up feeding my tiny baby whilst sitting on one of the toilets, weeping silently and feeling utterly humiliated.

A situation like this is enough to make anyone feel depressed, never mind the post-natal factors. It's also likely to make a mother feel reluctant about going out with her baby, so that she stays at home and is further depressed by the isolation. It's yet another divide for mothers to fall into. On the one hand, there's a strong lobby telling her she must breastfeed for the sake of the child; on the other, a society that humiliates her for doing so.

It doesn't even matter whether a woman's breasts are visible while she feeds. Just the idea of suckling is enough to send some people into paroxysms. I've been asked to leave a wine bar – or else breastfeed in the loo – although the people who complained (on their way out of the restaurant) would have needed X-ray eyes to see around the wall of our 'booth' and through the swathes of discreet clothing which were practically stifling the poor baby.

A New Zealand friend was flabbergasted that anyone should complain about such a natural and healthy activity. She claims her compatriots breastfeed quite confidently wherever they are. Besides, it's a great way to keep the baby quiet – something of which the whingeing public should perhaps be more mindful.

When grown men faint

Other women have told me about having to retreat to the back seat of their cars to feed their babies, while passers-by gawped in at the windows to their acute embarassment. But some women have literally nowhere to go. A manager of a hotel in Bloomsbury told me of how a woman had come in from the street to ask for a place where she could sit down and feed. He felt she was 'aggressive' and told her to try one of the bigger hotels. He also asked a guest at the hotel not to feed her baby in the restaurant, but to go upstairs to her bedroom – 'in order not to offend the other customers'.

According to Peggy Thomas of the Association of Breast-feeding Mothers – one of the groups behind the Babycare symbol scheme – women are often accused of 'breastfeeding aggressively'. It's a phrase which conjures up ludicrous images of mothers whipping out nipples and ramming them into the mouths of distraught infants. But to an alarming extent it reflects just how much some people do feel threatened and embarassed by women who breastfeed in public.

Patricia Hewitt, Neil Kinnock's press aide, caused such a stir by breastfeeding her baby in public that she made the diary column of the *Star* (17 October 1986). Apparently, Ms Hewitt went into the Labour Party headquarters to discuss a forth-coming by-election with party stalwarts from Liverpool. She took her baby with her, but when she fed the child, her colleagues were reported to be 'rather shaken'. Under the heading 'Pat keeps abreast of the news', there was this com-ment:

There is a division of opinion on this delicate matter of course. Some find it quite charming. Others however, tend to view the activity with profound discomfort. When Esther Rantzen did it, indeed, strong men practically fainted to the floor.

Peggy Thomas was told by a woman visitor – in her own home – to go out of the room and to feed her baby upstairs. 'I refused to go out of the room', she says, 'it's not like making love.' Yet that is precisely the trouble. In the public mind – conditioned by a flood of advertising images and pornography – breasts are inextricably and invariably associated with sex.

There's really only one way around that hurdle and that's to show the public that breasts are also about feeding babies. Peggy Thomas has a motto for new mothers: 'Sit there, smile – and do it.' She advocates discreet determination in the battle to re-educate the public on this issue:

I visualize a treaty: we won't be aggressive if you will be tolerant. I think it's nice to be discreet about breastfeeding. For instance, I suggest women pull up their T-shirts to feed rather than stripping off.

Which is what, she tells me, a group of women did do in Harrods as a protest after one mother was asked to leave the shop because she was breastfeeding.

Most mothers wouldn't dream of stripping off. They just want to be able to feed their babies without being treated like anti-social freaks. Perhaps when Britain has learned to cherish its children better and to value its mothers more, that happy time will come.

CHAPTER 8

Mad mothers – or a mad world?

Inheriting the earth

In some important respects, mothers and children have never had it so good. Compared with earlier generations and with many other countries we are almost free of the fear of death in childbirth and of losing children to disease. The quality of health and education available to us and our children would be the envy of many of our mothers and grandmothers. The very idea that we may be 'mad to be mothers' reflects the fact that modern women have an unprecedented degree of choice in the matter.

But these gains have cost us dear. We have all now to live with the knowledge that the same scientific advances that may have saved a baby's life at birth are part of a technology which gives us the potential to completely destroy our planet.

Modern life in all its sophistication feels as if it has slipped from our control. We are bringing up a new generation which is pessimistic and fatalistic about the future. One in three of British teenagers is worried about the threat of a nuclear holocaust and only one in ten thinks that governments will get together to work things out (*Guardian* 5/9/85).

Increasingly, the world of mothers and children – of survival and nurturing, of intuition and emotion – seems cut off from the 'real' world of mostly men with its wars, weapons and 'work'. The modern workplace where so many of us expend our energies according to distant dictates, continues to cut off the values of parenthood and home from the demands of production and profit.

Increasingly, mothers and children are caught in these divides. Mothers are a large proportion of the nation's paid workforce and as such they lead double lives. While a woman is at work she must be a 'closet mother', keeping quiet about the needs and values of home life. Yet from the perspective of home, the hustle and bustle of office life can look like a meaningless, mad scramble.

The gulf that often separates women with children from those without, shows just how difficult it has become to connect the two worlds. Mothers are saying that it is nearly impossible to explain to non-mothers what it is all about. Non-mothers are often baffled and bored by the world of mothers. If it's that hard for women to communicate about motherhood to other women, how much more dangerously is motherhood out on a limb from the values of the powers that be?

If we are to measure the priorities of our governments by the amounts of money they are prepared to invest, then the health and welfare of mothers and children is not a priority. We spend a smaller slice of our budget on health than any other advanced Western country. Yet we spend a bigger proportion on defence research and development than any other country barring the two super powers.

It is women who are the chief users of the health service, and as we have seen, thousands of babies die or suffer handicap each year as the result of lack of medical resources. Of course life has always been hazardous for babies, and motherhood has always made women more vulnerable. The difference is that today, while we have the potential to make life safer and better for both, our society is choosing not to do so.

Mothers, as the people who take most responsibility for the survival of children, directly feel the impact of such choices. As soon as the city mother steps out of her front door she is likely to feel the roar of traffic as a new threat, to taste the lead laden exhaust fumes with fresh apprehension, knowing what they could do to her child's developing brain.

154

As she goes shopping she is conscious of the food additives and colourings that manufacturers still routinely use despite our knowledge of the damage they can do to children. Pesticides, industrial wastes and radiation are now thought to damage women's reproductive systems and contaminate their breast milk.

After the Chernobyl accident mothers at my local mother and toddler group were talking about how the fallout of poisons might affect their children's health. One was worried that the organically grown vegetables from her garden might now be contaminated.

Another who was still breastfeeding her child felt she simply couldn't win. If she stopped breastfeeding and put him onto solids, that food might be contaminated. Yet if she carried on breastfeeding, her own milk might be contaminated by what she herself was eating. Neither of them had any confidence in the bland government reassurances that there was nothing to worry about.

A fate worse than birth?

The foreboding that many Western people feel about the future has enormous implications for motherhood. A lot of women are asking – is it fair, is it right, to bring a child into this kind of world?

It's not just the future which affects a woman's choice about motherhood, but the conditions under which mothers have to bring up their children in the present. Motherhood on its pedestal just doesn't match up with the reality.

It's obvious to any potential mother today that children are seen as a burden by most except their own families. She knows from witnessing the fate of friends who become mothers that the women who bear children somehow come to share their children's unesteemed position.

What harm may it do to our children to feel that our society cares more about power and possessions than it does for them and those who care for them? The soaring rate of child abuse in this country is at least in part an answer to that question.

Germaine Greer in her book *Sex and Destiny*, argues that Western society now offers women so few rewards for becoming mothers that our culture is in danger of dying out. She suggests that we have come to despise children and to fear fertility, believing that the greatest favour we can do for people in third world countries is to give them contraception:

One of the reasons why we so firmly believe that the only people with the right to want a child are its parents, is that we see quite clearly that bearing and raising a child is an ordeal. The individuals who we have painstakingly inducted into child-free society and established there, with a life style centred entirely upon achievement and self-gratification, have now to disrupt that pattern.

The sacrifice is enormous and they are to expect no reward or recompense. If the management of child-bearing in our society had actually been intended to maximize stress, it could hardly have succeeded better. The child-bearers embark on their struggle alone; the rest of us wash our hands of them.'

Since the mid-60s, women across Europe have been choosing to have fewer children, until we have reached the current situation where we are not replacing our own levels of population. So concerned is the Council of Europe about this that their European Population Committee has made an extensive study of the decline in fertility in the member states.

They reject the myths about low fertility – that it is caused by women going out to work, by contraception and abortion. On the contrary, womens' choices about children are determined by the values and structures of the society they live in. And our society does not set its values or order its institutions in ways which suit mothers. It is the uncertainty of employment, the high risks of relationships breaking down the threat of ecological disasters that are putting women off having more children.

According to Robert Cliquet of the Population and Family Study Centre in Brussels (Forum, EEC, Issue 3 1986), few, if any, Western European societies have managed to balance the needs of mothers with the demands of society. The Population Committee came to the conclusion that if society won't make it possible for women to have several children without being forced to sacrifice their freedoms and independence, then our populations will continue to steadily dwindle away. That's a prospect that has them seriously worried.

One world

To a large extent the system of Western values that fails to cherish its own mothers and children, is also responsible for a far more devastating unconcern for those of the developing world.

Just as in the UK it is women and children who are most vulnerable to cuts in health and social services, so it is the poorest women and children of the world, say UNICEF, who have borne the brunt of the world recession.

In 1985 UNICEF published their study of the recession from the point of view of the children of the world's poorest communities. It shows that social services are often the first things to be cut back in times of recession (and this one is the longest since the 1930s). Yet it is the poorest people who are dependent on these services. Just as it happens in the comparatively affluent West, the main impact of world recession is being borne by those least able to resist it.

It's by no means inevitable that the mothers and children of the world should suffer so harshly. When governments have the will, they find a way. Look at the war years in Britain, when despite shortages, health and nutrition amongst our children was better than it was in the years before and after the war. It's not a matter of how abundant resources may be, but of governments having the political will to make sure that resources are made available to mothers and children.

The Western world has managed to create a basic 'safety net' for the welfare of its people – although in Britain we have seen that net weakened and breached in recent years. And the enormous concern expressed by ordinary people in the various 'Aid' initiatives, starting with Band Aid and Live Aid, shows that most of us do care about the sufferings of other peoples and don't accept that it should go on.

UNICEF say that we could 'very cheaply', by introducing just a few simple measures of health and education, cut the rate of death, malnutrition and disabilities by half.

Every year, half a million women in the third world die from causes related to bearing children. For every woman who dies, many more suffer from damaged health. Fifteen million children are dying each year in the developing countries and infant mortality is up to eight times higher than in the West.

Women labour for long hours in developing countries, as well as bearing and caring for their children. The UN reports that women do nearly two-thirds of the world's work, but only earn a tenth of the world's income – while they are half of the world's people. These statistics link third world women to those of the West, whose work in motherhood and child-bearing remains invisible, undervalued and unpaid.

Mothers in developing countries are often the last to eat, eating the least. And while there is no comparison of the degree of malnutrition suffered by third world women, their problems are not different in kind from many of those in the 'rich' West. Even in the UK, as the Maternity Alliance have shown in their publication *Poverty in Pregnancy*, pregnant women who are on low wages or dependent upon benefits may not be able to afford even an 'adequate diet'.

Wherever they live in the world, mothers have the same kind of struggle – to make their men, their governments and their leaders acknowledge and support their rights. For women in the West this is a battle for a more just, equitable and fulfilling way of life. For third world women it is often a battle for survival too.

No matter how divided we may appear to be – in terms of our greater affluence – from the mothers of the third world, our interests are basically the same. We can hope that as we argue for improvements in the status of mothers in the West, our point of view will come to be represented in the decision making capitals of the world until leaders can no longer ignore the condition of the world's poorest mothers and children.

Reaction and action

Slowly but steadily, despite the setbacks of recent years, British mothers are making positive changes. As women we have become more independent and are refusing to accept the values that do not care for the welfare of children and their carers, that do not care for the earth we live on.

Reaction against the traditional role of mothers is turning into support and recognition of the fact that women are oppressed in motherhood. Mothers are becoming more vocal and active in fighting the assumptions and restrictions which limit their lives. Mothers and non-mothers are coming to understand what it is which divides them and to see that this divide is not in women's interests.

There is no going back from the changes in consciousness that the women's movement has brought about. Women have seen through the myths of idealized Motherhood, and in support groups and as friends are creating a true picture of what motherhood is really like.

Most of us do not accept that we should take entire responsibility for being childcarers, or bear the guilt when as mothers we are less than perfect. Most of us do not accept that the only way to be a 'normal' woman is to give birth, or that our childbearing function should define what we are as women.

Women are not waiting helplessly for disaster. The last decade has seen a great resurgence of the peace movement in which women, with and without children, have been to the forefront. Greenham Common has become an international symbol, while groups of 'parents for peace' have directly linked the issue of raising children with that of disarmament.

Women with varying viewpoints have taken up the issues

which they know to be affecting their position as mothers and the welfare of their children. As the Directory at the end of this book shows, women in the UK have continued to fight for better childcare and health, to preserve a system of benefits and to alleviate the stress and isolation which afflicts so many mothers.

In 1987 the Maternity Emergency campaign was launched, bringing together parents and non-parents from all over the country in defence of the rights of Britain's mothers – and by implication, of their children. Maternity Alliance, who launched the campaign, say they have been overwhelmed by the level of support from every quarter, and believe that this campaign is only the beginning of a change of national consciousness about mothering.

This fight is of more than simply practical relevance to mothers and children. It is an expression of a refusal to accept a system which devalues mothers and the values of parenthood while insisting that if they can't bring up their children without problems they are personally inadequate. It is part of a refusal to accept the long tradition of blaming mothers. As Adrienne Rich puts it in *Lies, Secrets and Silence*:

Once a woman has borne a child she is viewed as the primary and uttermost source of that child's good and evil, its survival, health, sanity and selfhood. Society . . . can still lay the blame for the waste of its young on the 'bad' mothers who have somehow failed to be superhuman, who have somehow failed to rear, in a callous and ruthless social order, well adjusted, obedient, achieving, non-alienated children.

If mothers really did have as much power and influence as the 'superhuman' myth would have it, our children probably would be happier, healthier people. Not that mothers have any automatic claim to some kind of mystical Life Force. After all, it is a mother who is responsible for the policies which so many other mothers in this country have objected to!

But there is no doubt that a greater valuing of women's

160

experience and point of view would make this a better and safer world. For many women, it is because they are so closely involved with children and their future that they are amongst the most active and committed of campaigners for a cleaner, safer, healthier and more just society.

Joan Ruddock of CND, speaking about ending nuclear power in Britain (October 1st, 1986), put it like this:

We do not inherit this earth from our parents. We borrow it from our children.

My baby works from nine-to-five . . .

In the sphere of paid work too, the traditional structures and priorities are being challenged. The old nine-to-five, five days a week, forty year long working life was constructed with the traditional male in mind. In the past, fathers 'worked' while mothers stayed at home.

But many of today's women have children as well as paid jobs, while a growing number of men are beginning to share in the care of their children. This great change in the profile of the British workforce demands a radical reappraisal of the relationship between home and paid work. The traditional ideology of work is also called into question by modern technology and the huge rise in unemployment.

What sense is there in keeping millions of people in poverty and enforced idleness, while the millions more in paid work would like to have more leisure time and more time for their families? Increasingly too, it is becoming clear that we won't get equal opportunities at work without changing the way that employees with children are treated.

Change is slowly but surely on its way. Many employers in this country are coming to see that it profits them to adjust the structures of work towards the needs of parents. According to the Equal Opportunities Commission, firms who give support to parents find it easier to recruit new staff. This is important in areas of skill shortages and in competitive businesses.

161

Employers are also realizing just how much more expensive it is to lose highly trained and skilled employees into motherhood. The Engineering Council has worked out that it costs a company up to £20,000 to lose a trained engineer, while the Inland Revenue say it costs them five years and £40,000 to train a tax inspector.

Male employees are also beginning to want a change in the way that home and work have been separated. Modern fathers are often present at the birth of their children, and almost all find they need to take some time off. Even in 1983 an EOC survey found that 94 per cent of fathers took some time off during their partner's pregnancies or in the post natal period. Not surprisingly, nine out of ten fathers strongly favoured the introduction of paid paternity leave.

The fairest and least descriminatory way of giving mothers and/or fathers a break from work to care for newborn or sick children is through parental leave. This was first introduced in Sweden and is now available in most parts of Europe. The only member country of the European Community to oppose parental leave – alas – is Britain.

But although British governments have not encouraged mothers back into paid work, there have been various positive initiatives from British employers. The banking world has taken the lead with their career break schemes, developed with the aim of hanging on to skilled and experienced 'high flyers'.

Companies like Thames TV have begun to make childcare payments to their employees. Other organizations, like *City Limits* magazine and the National Council for Voluntary Organizations, have their own parental leave schemes.

Job-sharing arrangements are increasingly common in this country and have proved they can be a great success. Not only does job sharing give workers the opportunity to work part-time, but the astute employer has learned that two heads can be better than one in terms of talent and experience within a job.

The traditionally rigid working day is being further undermined by flexitime working, now well established in the public sector. This allows employees to put in their hours of work at times best suited to themselves, within certain agreed limits.

In America, the State of New York has introduced 'V-time' – or voluntary reduction in working hours. This innovation allows employees to cut their hours (also taking a pro-rata cut in pay) by nearly a third over the period of about a year. Another way that hours of work are being juggled to give the employee a period of time off is the 'nine-day fortnight'.

Today's women now assume that they are going to be putting in a full lifetime of paid work. They want and need more flexibility at work, they want and need an end to discrimination against parents and part-timers. The current political climate isn't making it any easier for workers or employers to develop new ways of working, yet employment structures are slowly changing nonetheless.

Cherishing the future

In the private sphere too, the pressure upon men to share in the work of parenthood is growing. It is vital that men take on more, both at home and by adapting the world of work and politics to the needs of women. Fathers are still taking far less responsibility for childcare and housework than mothers, particularly for the more boring chores. But progress has been made.

Many men now accept in theory – if not in practise – that they should share in the bringing up of their children. Today's fathers are far more likely to change and clothe and feed children than those of the previous generation – and not many British parents will fail to notice that this year's Mothercare catalogue has a striking photograph of a man cradling two children on its front cover.

Some men are taking on the traditional female roles. And as more do so, the status of childminding is likely to improve. When men were secretaries, that was a good job to have. When more men are childcarers, we are more likely to have decent parental leave, nurseries, pro-parent initiatives at the workplace and a more child-friendly society.

And the more children that are brought up without reproducing the old divides between male and female, powerful and powerless, child and adult, non-parent and mother, the more likely we are to have a generation who can live complete lives.

Having children is in itself a part of a healing process. Motherhood connects us to the women of the past and to generations to come. In bringing up children we are constantly having to give birth to parts of ourselves that we didn't know existed, or that we had denied. Motherhood confirms our strength and creativity and affirms our faith in the future.

We need that future to be one which deeply values and respects women and children, that values us for our humanity and not for our position on the ladder of production and profit. We need that future to be one in which all people can share in the bringing up of children, in caring and providing for them so that they can achieve their full potential.

We need that future to be one in which we can love and enjoy our children because they are – for many of us – the best and most cherished parts of our lives.

Motherhood will never be easy. But in a saner world, we don't have to be mad to be mothers.

Directory of useful addresses

All over the country women and women's organizations are working in their various ways to make life happier and healthier for mothers and children. This directory is by no means an exhaustive index, but it does include some of the chief groups and interesting new initiatives which I came across in the course of writing this book.

The groups are listed under headings which indicate their main concern or area of interest: from therapy for mothers to mothers' rights to childlessness. I hope every woman will find something helpful here.

The directory is offered with apologies for the inevitable ommissions (much mutual support between mothers goes unlisted anywhere), and with thanks for the ideas contributed to the book by these groups.

Breastfeeding

Three-quarters of today's mothers breastfeed their babies, yet nursing mothers still need plenty of moral support and in-formation.

The Association of Breastfeeding Mothers (ABM) began in 1980 as a small support group for nursing mothers. It has now spread across the UK as a self-help network with counsellors, a newsletter, and book sales service. It costs £6 to join.

ABM,
131 Mayow Road,
London SE26 4HZ.
Tel: 01 778 4769

The La Lèche League also provides breastfeeding help and information:

La Lèche League,
BM 3424,
London WC1 N 3XX.
Tel: 01 404 5011

Childcare

Changes in society and in family life mean that young children may be living in isolation as never before. Women are under great pressure to stay at home to look after their children. Yet safe care, play and learning is as good for children as it is beneficial to women who cannot hope for equality without it.

The National Child Care Campaign (NCCC) works for government recognition for the needs of mothers and children in childcare. They are actively opposed to the run-down or closure of the already inadequate facilities, and campaign for the rights of all children under twelve, regardless of race, disability, gender or economic background. The NCCC also publishes newsletters, information and advice leaflets and offers support to parents and staff in fighting cuts in childcare.

NCCC,
Wesley House,
70 Great Queen Street,
London WC2B 5AX.
Tel: 01 405 5617/8

The Inland Revenue's decision to tax workplace nurseries not only put many parents badly out of pocket but threatens the closure of nurseries. The Workplace Nurseries Campaign is a voluntary group working to abolish this tax, to defend existing nurseries and to develop other forms of employment-related childcare. They offer a useful information pack and newsletter.

Workplace Nurseries Campaign,
Room 205,
South Bank House,
Black Prince Road,
London SE1 7SJ.
Tel: 01 582 7199/587 1546

The Pre-School Playgroups Association is a voluntary association of mother and toddler groups, playgroups and families of under-fives. Through community groups they encourage parents to understand and provide for the development of their small children. They offer help in setting up groups, and hold courses and conferences. The PPA also encourages research and publishes information including 'Contact' and 'Under Five' for playgroups and parents.

PPA,
Alford House,
Aveline Street,
London SE11 5DH.
Tel: 01 582 8871

Children in danger

Although the majority of our 15 million children grow up in loving homes, many thousands of others are being damaged by fear, violence and suffering. The National Children's Home (NCH) says that today's children are as vulnerable as they have ever been in its 117-year history.

We may have eradicated many Victorian evils of exploitation, but instead our children face the modern dangers of sexual abuse, drugs, divorce and sharpening poverty.

In response, the NCH has moved forward from its residential tradition to launch a wide variety of projects. Where families are divided by divorce it provides counselling and conciliation services. It runs family support services and centres for lone parents which provide a form of training for parenthood. The NCH also campaigns for schools to prepare children for marriage and parenthood, and lobbies for government support for poor families.

'Children Today' is a factfile about children in Britain and Northern Ireland which leaves no room for complacency. For this booklet and other services contact:

National Children's Home,
85 Highbury Park,
London N5 1UD.

The National Society for the Prevention of Cruelty to Children (NSPCC) fields child protection teams which work closely with local authorities and specialist agencies. They also maintain child abuse registers for local social services and health agencies, and have a variety of other community-based services for children and parents. The NSPCC urges anyone who suspects a child is being ill-treated to contact them.

NSPCC,
67 Saffron Hill,
London EC1N 8RS.
Tel: 01 242 1626

The Children's Legal Centre (CLC) is concerned with law and policy as it affects young people. It believes children should be respected as individuals with a right to a say in the decisions which affect their lives. Its services include advice, information, a monthly bulletin 'Childright' and a variety of publications of interest to anyone who works with children.

CLC,
20 Compton Terrace,
London N1 2UN.
Tel: 01 359 6251

Child safety

Accidents are the commonest cause of death amongst toddlers and older children. Four children are killed in accidents every day, and one in three of all patients coming to hospital accident and emergency departments is a child. Every year, one child in five has an accident at home or in the road which is serious enough for hospital or GP treatment.

Not all of these are preventable in a world full of dangers for unsteady and curious children. But there are safety guidelines which do help.

'Keep Them Safe', a free booklet from the Child Accident Prevention Trust recommends safety guidelines with special reference to safety equipment. Health visitors should be able to provide copies, or write to Keep Them Safe, Dept HS3, 13–39 Standard Road, London NW10 6HD.

The Health Education Council has also produced a booklet called 'Play It Safe: A Guide to Preventing Children's Accidents.' Free from the HEC, 78 New Oxford Street, London WC1A 1AH.

Disability

The Voluntary Council for Handicapped Children (VCHC) offers a comprehensive information and advisory service covering all aspects of disability for statutory and voluntary agencies as well as parents. It publishes fact sheets and information on what's happening in this field.

VCHC,
8 Wakely Street,
London EC1V 7QE.
Tel: 01 278 9441

Sisters Against Disablement (SAD) is a feminist group for women with disabilities.

SAD,
c/o Mayrav Dover,
241 Albion Road,
London N16.
Tel' 01 241 2263

Family support

'The joys of parents are secret and so are their griefs and fears.' Francis Bacon's saying has become a motto of the Parent Network, which aims to dissolve parental isolation and inexperience through a national network of parent support groups. Founded in 1986, they hope through their Parent Link programme to help parents to share their experiences of family life and develop relationship skills under the guidance of trained group leaders.

The Parent Network,
44-46 Caversham Road,
London NW5 2DS.
Tel: 01 485 8535

Family Network runs telephone help lines for people experiencing difficulties within their families. Set up in 1979 by the National Children's Homes, volunteers offer a listening and referral service, and some Family Network centres have drop-in centres, self-help groups and counselling.

Family Network,
85 Highbury Park,
London N5 1UD.
Tel: 01 226 2033

Lone parents

One million of Britain's seven million families are one-parent families. The vast majority of these have lost a partner through death or desertion. Their children are no more disturbed or delinquent than those in families with married parents – contrary to widely believed fictions. Lone parents, however, can feel very isolated in our couple-oriented society, and may face great financial, legal and housing problems.

Gingerbread is a self-help, mutual support association for one-parent families with a national network of some 400 groups and over 13,000 members. It also has advice and information services, a quarterly magazine and a holiday organization.

Gingerbread,
35 Wellington Street,
London WC2E 7BN.
Tel: 01 240 0953

The National Council for One Parent Families (NCOPF) offers help and advice to lone parents and single pregnant women. It gives free and confidential legal advice, pregnancy counselling, help with housing problems, social security, taxation and maintenance. It represents parents at appeals and may help to keep children out of council care. It is also a campaigning pressure group with its own information office.

NCOPF,
255 Kentish Town Road,
London NW5 2LX.
Tel: 01 267 1361

Mothers' mutual support

At the end of the day it is women with children who are best placed to understand what other mothers may be going through. Mothers help and support each other from the most informal levels to the countrywide organizations like the National Childbirth Trust (NCT). Although most people think of it chiefly in terms of their classes in preparation for childbirth, the most rapidly growing area of the NCT's work is in post-natal support groups.

NCT's 'befrienders' are mothers without formal training who offer support to other mothers, easing the isolation that new mums often feel.

NCT,
9 Queensborough Terrace,
London W2.
Tel: 01 221 3833.

Mothers' rights

Mothers' rights are in crisis in Britain with cuts in benefits and erosion of employment rights which leave mothers more vulnerable than they have been for seventy years.

The Maternity Alliance is an organization which campaigns for improvements in rights and services for parents and babies. In April it launched the broadly based Maternity Emergency Campaign to highlight the crisis and to press for change.

Maternity Alliance,
59-61 Camden High Street,
London NW1.
Tel: 01 388 6337

The Equal Opportunities Commission also takes up cases of mothers whose rights may have been violated. The EOC has information on the innovations which employers are beginning to make in the field of parental leave and in more flexible employment policies suited to parents.

EOC,
Overseas House,
Quay Street,
Manchester M3 3HN.

Lesbian mothers often face the loss of custody of their children. The Rights of Women group (ROW) has a lesbian custody worker.

ROW,
52-54 Featherstone Street,
London EC1.
Tel: 01 251 6576

Parents under stress

Today's mothers are under so much stress that post-natal illness afflicts up to half of all women with young children.

172

There are now self-help groups across the country to help prevent and alleviate such difficulties.

Association for Post Natal Illness,
c/o 7 Gowan Avenue,
London SW6.
Tel: 01 831 8996

Parents Anonymous,
6-9 Manor Gardens,
London N7.
Tel: 01 263 5672/8918

Poverty

Millions of mothers and children are living on the breadline. Record numbers depend on supplementary benefits.

The Child Poverty Action Group (CPAG) actively helps families to get their full entitlement to benefits, and educates politicians and the public about the extent and impact of poverty in the UK. Its welfare benefits guides explain the social security rules in plain English. Demand for these is at 'best-seller' level, with sales of over 70,000 a year.

The CPAG has a free information, advisory and advocacy service, the Citizens' Rights Office (CRO) which helps claimants with welfare benefit difficulties. The CRO specializes in 'test cases' to challenge the law. CPAG also carries out research on poverty, suggests alternative policies and runs courses for advice givers.

CPAG,
1 Macklin Street,
London WC2B 5NH.
Tel: 01 242 3225/9149

Therapy for mothers

Such is the gap between women's expectations and the realities of motherhood, that increasingly mothers seem to be turning to therapy for a deeper understanding of their situation.

The Women's Therapy Centre offers workshops for women who are concerned about being childless, who lose their children or their options to have children as they grow older, and for women who have had abortions. For mothers they offer workshops on pregnancy and giving birth, and on bringing up children of mixed race.

Women's Therapy Centre,
6 Manor Gardens,
London N7 6LA.
Tel: 01 263 6200

Exploring Parenthood is a national organization which runs workshops to give 'a chance to explore the problems and pleasures of being a parent'. It was founded in 1983 as a charitable trust by a child psychotherapist and a family therapist.

The workshops are led by experts from the fields of family, child, adolescent and adult development, and they focus on the everyday issues and challenges of parenthood. Parents are also offered help and advice in setting up local support groups and networks. There is a quarterly newsletter.

Exploring Parenthood,
Omnibus Workspace,
39-41 North Road,
London N7 9DP.
Tel: 01 607 9647.

Racism

The Commission for Racial Equality (CRE) is a good source of information and contacts among ethnic minority organizations for parents who are concerned about how racism may affect their families. It provides legal advice and undertakes investigations. The CRE has much free literature available, including 'Caring for Under-Fives in a Multi-Racial Society' and 'The Ante-Natal Language Kit'.

CRE,
Elliot House,
10-12 Allington Street,
London SW1E 5EH.
Tel: 01 828 7022

Under fives

VOLCUF is the Voluntary Organizations Liaison Council for the Under-Fives which believes it's vital to bring together the people and organizations committed to young children and families. Its aim is to improve services, facilities and training in the care of small children. VOLCUF is actively anti-racist.

Through workshops, conferences and research seminars they provide a forum for new developments. The organization has a collection of books and journals available to members. VOLCUF's quarterly newsletter *Co-ordinate* is a valuable resource with news of national and local developments as they affect the under-fives.

VOLCUF,
c/o Thomas Coram Foundation,
40 Brunswick Square,
London WC1N 1AZ.
Tel: 01 278 3459/3450/8365

Women without children

Motherhood is a matter which affects all women, whether they have children or not. For infertile women, the National Association for the Childless (NAC) provides support and information. Its members are drawn from the medical profession working with infertility, as well as from infertile people.

NAC has a newsletter and pamphlets like 'Unfocused Grief', about the emotional impact of infertility.

NAC,
318 Summer Lane,
Birmingham B19 3RL.
Tel: 021 359 4887

Other women are childless by choice. The British Organization of Non-Parents (BON) tries to counter the social pressures to have children by drawing attention to the benefits of a childless life. BON holds meetings and publishes a newsletter.

BON,
BM Box 5866,
London WC1N 3XX

'Working' mothers

Is there a 'working' mother (all mothers are working mothers) in existence who doesn't feel torn between her job and her child? If so, she'll have no need of the Working Mothers' Association, which now has over fifty groups nationwide to provide mutual support, advice on childcare and information on local facilities for mothers.

The Association holds scheduled monthly meetings and has a telephone enquiry service.

Working Mothers' Association,
7 Spencer Walk,
London SW15 1PL.
Tel: 01 788 2565.

Further Reading

Alone of All her Sex: The Myth and the Cult of the Virgin Mary, Marina Warner, Weidenfeld and Nicholson 1976.
Babies and Money, Jo Roll, Family Policy Studies Centre, 1986.
A Celebration of Babies, Sally Emerson, Blackie 1986.
The Experience of Infertility, Naomi Pfeffer and Anne Woollett, Virago 1983.
The Feminine Mystique, Betty Friedan, Penguin/Pelican 1982.
Femininity, Susan Brownmiller, Hamilton, 1984.
From Here to Maternity, Ann Oakley, Penguin 1979.
The Good Mother, Sue Miller, Gollancz 1986.
Housewife, Ann Oakley, Pelican 1976.
Inequalities in Health (Black Report), Black et al, Penguin 1982.
Inventing Motherhood, Ann Dally, Burnett 1982.
Man Made Language, Dale Spender, Routledge 1985.
Maternity Rights Handbook, Ruth Evans and Lyn Durward, Penguin 1984.
Miscarriage, Ann Oakley et al., Collins/Fontana 1984.
Of Woman Born, Adrienne Rich, Virago 1977.
On Being a Mother, Georgina Boulton, Tavistock 1983.
On Lies, Secrets and Silence, Adrienne Rich, Norton 1979.
The London Women's Handbook, Produced and published by the GLC Women's Committee, 1986.
Pregnancy, Gordon Bourne, Pan 1975.
The State of the World's Children 1986, OUP/UNICEF 1985.
Sex and Destiny: The Politics of Human Fertility, Germaine Greer, Secker and Warburg 1984.
Sex and Love, Sue Cartledge and Joanna Ryan (eds). The Women's Press 1983.
Why Children? Stephanie Dowrick and Sibyl Grundberg (eds), The Women's Press 1980.